I0740634

Nora Vynne

The Blind Artist's Pictures and Other Stories

ISBN/EAN: 9783337331085

Printed in Europe, USA, Canada, Australia, Japan

Cover: Foto ©Thomas Meinert / pixelio.de

More available books at **www.hansebooks.com**

Nora Vynne

The Blind Artist's Pictures and Other Stories

THE
BLIND ARTIST'S PICTURES;

AND OTHER STORIES

BY

NORA VYNNE,

Author of "Honey of Aloes," "Mr. Jenkins' Bargain," &c., &c.

LONDON:

JARROLD & SONS, 10 & 11, WARWICK LANE, E.C.

1893.

Dedication.

TO

JOHN STRANGE WINTER

(Mrs. Arthur Stannard),

TO WHOSE

KINDLY HELP AND ENCOURAGEMENT

I OWE VERY MUCH

MORE THAN IT WOULD BE POSSIBLE TO SAY

IN A DEDICATION,

I DEDICATE MY FIRST BOOK.

N. V.

CONTENTS.

	PAGE
THE BLIND ARTIST'S PICTURES	9
THE MAIDEN LOVED OF CLEOMENES	75
AN UNNOTICED INCIDENT	105
MISS MAY'S GUEST	145
JOHN O'NEAL'S HONOUR	191
BELIEVE IT NOW	205
ZAHNAHA'S LOVER	243
LADY ATHERTON'S SACHET	255
THE ADMIRAL'S GOOD NATURE	283
AN UGLY LITTLE WOMAN	319
"ANDREW PATERSON"	333

THE BLIND ARTIST'S PICTURES.

The Blind Artist's Pictures.

CHAPTER I.

A PHILANTHROPIC SCHEME.

SERENA MAULDEN and Ferdinand Brail were very dear friends, in spite of some fifty-five years difference in their ages, or perhaps all the more on account of that difference. He was a great artist—might have been one of the greatest in Europe perhaps—only long ago, when he had been young and strong, he had let himself get thoroughly wet out sketching, trying to catch the wonderful shades of a Cumberland thunderstorm, and, with the almost impious carelessness of youth, had taken no account of it, and sat for hours in his wet clothes; the result was an attack of rheumatic fever, which left him a cripple.

This had hampered his studies, but could not destroy his genius. Travel was next door to an impossibility to him, and hard work an utter impossibility. Yet spending all his life extended on a sofa, he still had painted, and painted gloriously. Sea pieces generally, horrible wild storms, so fierce, and so awful, that, looking on them, one almost felt the agony of the drowning sailors; or stern rock-bound coasts, with great futile waves, dashing in helpless anger against them, or hurling some stately ship to destruction.

Sometimes—but only sometimes—he painted portraits, painted them with wonderful truth and vivacity, but it was now and then said, half in wonder, and half in jest, that those whose portraits he had painted were invariably unlucky.

He had painted Serena Maulden's portrait eight years ago, when she was a light-hearted girl in her first season—one of the pets of society—not a great beauty, but so sweet, people said, so "nice." A girl with no sarcasm in her whole composition, only pleasant, frank common-sense, and a very pretty, gentle manner. She had made a bewitching subject; the portrait was to have been her father's present to her husband on her marriage, but before the portrait was finished the lover had been found utterly worthless, and had fled in fear and shame from all who knew him. So long as it was possible Serena was true to him: standing up for him against overwhelming proof, and speaking brave words in his defence—brave and loyal words; but they sounded terribly pathetic to those who knew only too well that he had neither cared, nor dared to defend himself.

At last, when she realised that her late lover

neither valued nor desired her fidelity, she submitted; but she believed her life was over. She made no show of anger or sorrow; she simply bade a kind farewell to society, walked out of it backwards, as it were, curtseying at the door, and lived a quiet life in her own home.

Perhaps no one but Ferdinand Brail ever knew what she suffered at the time when she heard the evil news, and through the many days which followed, while—vainly certain that her lover would clear himself—she had insisted on having the picture finished. They never spoke of her lover then, though she had often talked about him before with the sweet confidence of a young girl towards a very old man whom she loves and trusts, but at last, when she begged him to send home the picture as it was, for she did not want ever to see it again, he knew what that meant. He said nothing, except that he hoped she would still come to see him often, for he was lonely and liked to talk to her, and lame and unable to come to her.

So, after she had taken leave of society, Serena went often to the old man's studio. The two grew to be very firm friends, and had countless pleasant talks together, but they never spoke of her lover once during the eight years of their friendship.

Serena had lived the last few years almost entirely alone. Her sisters had grown up and married, and were with their husbands, one of whom was a governor of an insignificant far-off colony ; another, an exceptional Irish landlord, who lived on his estate on good terms with his tenants, in some place with an unpronounceable name, at the extreme left-hand corner of the map ; the third, a Midland squire, devoted to hunting and drainage. Her father, who divided his time pretty equally among his four daughters, was at present visiting the colonial couple.

A few years after Serena had so hopelessly lost her lover, an affliction even greater than his lameness had befallen her old friend. His eyesight slowly left him, and his painting was at an end. Still, he had one consolation left: he could not paint pictures on canvas, but he could paint them in words—could paint them until his hearers saw them almost as vividly as he did, and this was a pleasure that could never leave him.

While he could yet see, he had seen the bitterness of sorrow pass away from Serena's face, leaving it still sweet and fair, with all life's possibilities yet in it ; and when her face had slowly faded from his sight he could still hear her pleasant voice and sweet low laugh, and she made the chief figure in many a dream picture.

To-day they were sitting together in the big bow window of the room which had been the studio—that is, she was sitting on a low chair, and he was reclining on a wicker American sofa ; a bright silk drapery was thrown over him, leaving his arms and shoulders free ; beside him was a low table containing the breakfast equipage, some magazines, and a volume of Morris's poems.

Serena had been reading aloud, and Mr. Brail had not been paying the least attention; he had come out with utterly irrelevant remarks upon the state of the weather, and the state of the political atmosphere, the doctor's last prescription, and the last new music, during the most tragic passages; and between the most telling lines—

"It is no use," he said at last, "I can't listen. I have been thinking about women, and I am cross —naturally.   My dear, do you look nice this afternoon?"

"Yes," she answered promptly.   "I look very nice indeed.   I have my newest hat on, and my newest hat is very becoming; then my gloves match it perfectly, and all the buttons fasten. Generally the first button of my gloves will not fasten, but these will, because they are a very good pair of gloves."

Mr. Brail coloured with pleasure in spite of his eighty-one years.   It was just like his Serena to put on her prettiest clothes to visit him, although he was blind and could not see her.

He took hold of one of the well-shaped hands as if to verify her assertion concerning the buttons.

"Serena, my dear," he said, after a pause, "as I said, I have been thinking about women."

"Well, dear, what about them?"

"They are so terribly conscious of their femininity;

they never lose sight of it for a moment. They forget that they are humanities, they forget they are immortalities, because they will never lose sight of their femininity. And the worst of it is," he went on inconsequently, "you are as bad as any of them."

"Yes, have I been giving an example lately?"

"Of course; that was what set me thinking—what you told me last time you were here."

"I forget.   What is it?"

"Of course you forgot the incident, but I remember it, and have been seeing most frightful pictures ever since. Let me remind you. You were coming from Streatham Common to Kensington, and you had to change carriages at Clapham Junction. As far as I remember it is a great misfortune to have to change carriages at Clapham Junction."

"Yes," said Serena, "no matter where you want to go you have to wait twenty-five minutes for your train."

"It was two thirty-five in the afternoon. You knew there was no train to Kensington for some time, but you knew also that by walking across to Battersea you could catch a Richmond train which stopped at Addison Road."

"Yes," said Serena. "I thought myself very clever for knowing that."

"As you were going down the steps to the underground passage, you heard behind you the following fragment of dialogue:—' When is the next to Kensington?' 'Three-fifteen, sir.' 'Three-fifteen? Oh Lord!' Half turning, you saw a young man—you said a 'masher,' but I shan't encourage you in talking slang—a young man standing in an attitude of dismal consternation as the stolid ticket collector turned away from him to the other passengers. Instead of charitably imparting your little piece of useful knowledge, you walked off by yourself, leaving him still in consternation."

"Well," she said, laughing, "was it so very wrong?"

"Yes—very wrong indeed. Just consider; that young man may have been a very hard-up young man—a respectable 'unemployed.' His clothes count for nothing, you know; he may have had on his best because he had pawned his second suit; he may have been on his way to apply for an appointment and lost it through being late. Serena, that young man may be starving in a garret now through your—femininity!"

"Let us hope not," said Serena.

"Or, perhaps, he was on his way to make up a quarrel with his *fiancée.* 'Dearest, meet me at three o'clock, and I will explain all,' he had entreated, and she had consented. Three o'clock comes— there I see her, pacing up and down the appointed spot; at five minutes past three she is impatient; at ten minutes past three she is tearful; at a quarter past three she is angry; at twenty minutes past three she has gone off in a rage, and accepted the other fellow!"

"I should suggest that if she is so quick-tempered he is best without her."

"Ah, but perhaps it was something quite different," said Mr. Brail promptly; "he may have been a married man with a wife and family, an aged mother, and an infirm mother-in-law depending on him. He has a good business, but a temporary embarrassment obliges him to ask a loan of his rich uncle. 'I'm not sure if I shall want it,' he says, 'but, if I do, I will let you know on Friday by three o'clock.' 'All right,' says the uncle, 'you shall have it if you want it.' Three o'clock comes: the uncle, a lawyer, has meanwhile received a letter begging him to go down at once to Devonshire to make the will of a rich client. He waits, packed bag in hand. Three o'clock comes, no nephew. 'I'll give him five minutes grace,' says the uncle. Gives him five—gives him ten—fifteen. 'Well,' says he at last, 'a man coming for money was never known to be late. It is clear my nephew's affairs are all right.' So he goes; and that young man bolts to America, and his wife and family are thrown on the parish."

"Let us hope it isn't so bad as all that," said Serena. "After all, perhaps, he was only going to Kensington to have afternoon tea with his aunt."

"Perhaps," admitted Mr. Brail gloomily, "and in that case he very likely caught such a cold waiting among the draughts at Clapham Junction that he will go into consumption and die miserably a year or two hence. But you didn't tell him of that train at Battersea; you did not think of all the awful possible consequences, because your mind was filled with the thought that you were a young lady, and he was a gentleman."

"Excuse the correction, but I said a 'masher.' It was vulgar, I know, but that was what I said."

"I accept the correction, my dear, but what does it lead to?"

"Why this: if I had been sure he was a gentleman I would have spoken, because I should have been understood; but what if he had not been a gentleman? When I had told him the train, the next thing would have been to tell him the way—the way I was going myself in fact—and his inference——"

She would have left her sentence unfinished even if Mr. Brail had not interrupted her.

"There—that is just what I mean. You thought you would be misjudged. Well, what matter? you should not have thought of opinions, you should have thought of consequences. Your mind was full of femininity, when you should have thought, here are two human beings, and one of them can help the other. A woman should remember after all that a man is a fellow-creature, and be ready to help him a little—even unconventionally."

"I don't quite know what you mean by unconventional, there are so many degrees of queerness."

"Go on. If I could see your face I should know exactly what you meant to say. I almost know from your voice."

"Well, I know I should never do anything I thought wrong" (she said this with the most easy frankness imaginable, as if such knowledge were a very common thing, and quite certain not to be mistaken); "at least, I think I know that, but I should not mind doing anything strange or unusual if it were for a good purpose, to please you, for instance."

"Thank you. Do you know Mr. Earne—Stan Earne?"

"No; except from the newspapers."

"I painted his portrait."

"Then I should like to know him, because you only paint nice people."

"You know what some people say," he said with a half-sad smile, "that I only paint unfortunate people."

"It was fortunate that you painted me," she said pleasantly, "for I should never have known you else."

"I've seen a good deal of Earne ever since I painted him, and that was nine years ago—just before he went in for politics—and he has never been unfortunate that I know of until now."

"What has happened to him now?"

"The friend he trusted most has betrayed him."

"Oh!" she exclaimed with painfully intense sympathy.

"Well, the girl to whom he was engaged has jilted him. Does it sound better or worse that way?"

"It sounds very bad either way."

"Very bad! that is what one says of the toothache, 'very bad.' It is fatal!"

"Fatal?"

"Yes, it is killing Stanway Earne."

"Impossible! men don't die of love!"

"Not in the ordinary way, of course: there will be no funeral; his friends won't go into mourning, his heir won't rejoice, but the Stanway Earne that might have been—that God meant to be—is dying!"

"Oh, but that needn't be."

"No, but it is. You say you knew him from the newspapers; then you knew what all friends and foes alike knew of him—that he was that *rara avis* in modern politics—a politician with courtesy and conscience; a clever, earnest, honest young man, giving his whole life to his country in the cause he deemed best. That was the living man—the dead one, the corpse that will not be buried, will be an idle, dissipated, hopeless cynic, with no purpose in his life and no faith in himself."

"This is horribly sad."

"It is true, though. This girl's faithlessness has overthrown all his beliefs—he seems to care for nothing; he neglects his duties and shuns his friends; he is getting into trouble with his constituents. I can't enter into details, but he is going to the bad as fast as he can; he drinks—he never did that before—and I am afraid he is trying to forget his troubles in follies."

" He must be very weak."

" No—only very impressionable. Some men are like musical instruments that must give out some sound, and if God does not play on them the devil will. The devil has got hold of poor Earne just now, and is making very broken music."

" Can nothing be done ? "

" Of course, or I should not tell you all this. You can do something—everything. You can make him forget his unhappy first love in a happy second. You can make love to him courageously, and I am sure successfully. Well, how astonished you are looking ! I can hear it in your silence ! "

" That would indeed be unusual."

" Certainly, but you can't say it would be wrong."

" It isn't likely I could make him care for me."

" You must chance that ; your business is simply to try to make him."

" It would be so unwomanly."

" Of course, but it would save the life of that Stanway Earne I was speaking of."

She saw now what he had meant by his denunciation of female femininity.

" But he is a politician, and I don't agree with his politics."

" Look at it in this way—my way. I never understood politics, and I never could see that one party was better than the other, but a certain number of men manage by all pulling separate ways to get the state governed somehow. Now it is obvious, if wise and good men predominate, it is well : if foolish and bad men, it is ill for the country. Now if you save Stan Earne, that is one good man more ; if you don't, there is one good man less, and one bad one more. You see he counts double that way as they do in divisions. As to party, I can't see for the life of me what it matters which side a good man works on ; wherever he is he is bound to do good.

" But, Mr. Brail, you said he drank, and to marry a drunkard ! Think of it."

" I have thought of it. My child, if you make this effort you are doing a very brave thing. If you succeed, you, a woman, may feel you have served your country in saving this man's life for her service, but if you fail your own life will be a ruin."

" And you ask me to do it. You, who love me ! "

" I ask you because I love you, because I want you to do a noble and beautiful thing. Will you not save your brother unless you can do so without risk ? Does the fireman think how he may be maimed or scarred or killed when he rushes into the fire to save a life ? My child, don't think I don't know what a great thing I ask of you, but who so fit as you to do it ? "

She knew what he meant, that she, having lost her own chance of happiness long ago, could safely take her failed life in her hands and use it for this purpose. The purpose looked grand and noble, as her eager, white-haired old friend described it, and, after all, why should not one as well as the other of two humanities—two immortalities as he phrased it—try to win love?

She stood considering, he reached out and took her hand. "I will think of it," she said slowly.

At this moment the servant announced, "Mr. Earne, sir."

"Unfair," murmured Serena, trying to draw her hand away. "I have not thought."

But Mr. Brail held her hand fast, a smile of good-natured triumph on his face.

"Here you are at last, Earne, we are going to have some breakfast and were waiting for you."

"We!" At the plural pronoun Mr. Earne stopped short, and glanced suggestively at the door as it closed behind him.

"Oh, I didn't expect—I mean I told you I would come this morning, so I called on my way home."

Mr. Earne hesitated and spoke with such evident and painful embarrassment that Serena looked up quickly to see what was the matter.

The matter was very plain indeed. It was now quite half-past eleven in the morning, and Mr. Earne was in evening dress, in yesterday's evening dress. His linen was crumpled and soiled, his hair disarranged, his eyes red-rimmed and sleepy. He had the wretched and unmistakeable look of a man who has not washed since yesterday's dinner-time, and there was a blackguardly blue shadow on his chin and lip. It is appalling what tremendous advance a usually well-shaved beard can make in twenty-four hours.

To make the matter worse, when he so unexpectedly found himself in the presence of a person who could see and note his appearance, Mr. Earne was so overcome with shame as to be almost speechless.

It was fortunate that Mr. Brail, fearing lest Serena in consequence of their late conversation should feel shy or awkward, talked for all three at first.

Presently, after he had introduced his guest, and appealed to Serena to pour out the tea, he thought it time to set the others talking.

"Miss Maulden is a young lady who puts on her prettiest hat to come to see a blind man," he said. "I am sure she looks charming in all her hats, but I mention the fact because it is characteristic."

Mr. Earne had been shrinking back in a big chair with his eyes on the ground; now for the first time he raised them, and looked across at her, not to see the hat, but to implore her not to betray him, not to let it be known that he had taken advantage of his friend's blindness to appear before him in a state so plainly showing how the past night had been spent.

"I think Miss Maulden is right to put on that

hat on every opportunity," he said with a hurried effort to be common-place.

Serena was sorry for him; he had no more idea of the hat than he had of what he was saying, and the forced gaiety of his words contrasted very painfully with his sleepless eyes and intensely humiliated expression. Mr. Brail went on.

"Of course she always looks nice. Ah, what a while it is since I saw her, or you either for that matter! How is he looking, Serena?"

There was a pause. Serena felt herself turn scarlet. Mr. Earne again raised his eyes to hers, this time with no request in them, only very bitter shame. It flashed into Serena's mind that she was beginning to make love very desperately indeed, since she began with a downright lie.

"Well?" said Mr. Brail.

"I think," began Serena, and stopped. Poor girl, she came up to her lie gallantly enough, but she couldn't get over it. Earne saw and told it himself.

"I don't think it is fair to beguile your friends into personal remarks, Mr. Brail. I fancy I am looking as well as I know how. I must go now. I only looked in in passing to see how you were getting on."

"No, stay; I like to have you loitering in my rooms. I know you are a busy man with important duties, social and political, exacting constituents, and endless business that I don't understand. So

I like you to neglect all that and come here to amuse me; it makes me feel important."

Earne laughed. "I have important duties, as you phrase it, this afternoon, some Bill about railways or drainage, that my dear Ledway constituents have gone mad over. I think I will come here and read Morris to you."

"Serena," said Mr. Brail gravely, "I should like to know what you think of that suggestion."

"I think it is very good-natured," she replied in the same tone, "but you know my thoughts don't matter. Opinions don't matter; we must consider consequences. Mr. Earne, I have been having a lesson on consequences this morning. If you don't attend to the Ledway Drainage Bill, when the hot weather comes scarlet fever will break out, and all the good people in Ledway will probably die, and all the disagreeable people will probably recover. Or, to make the picture more touching——"

"No, no," interrupted Mr. Earne, "there is no danger. It is a new harbour they want." He felt deeply grateful to the girl who was shielding him so good-naturedly.

"That is rather worse. Imagine a homeward-bound ship, containing the long-looked-for father of a very large family, the consumptive daughter of an aged widow who had been a trip to the Cape, the young lawyer to whom the clergyman's eldest daughter is engaged, and all the sweethearts of all the Ledway mill-girls. The ship is in full sail, a sudden wind rises—no time to take in sail. The vessel is dashed against the rocks and all on board perish, because you were here reading Morris when you should have been attending to the Ledway Harbour Bill."

Mr. Earne rose with a laugh, natural and pleasant this time. "I will go home this moment and get a few hours sleep, and then it shan't be my fault, Miss Maulden, if the Ledwayites are not a little nearer towards getting their harbour this afternoon."

"Now, I should like to know," said Mr. Brail, "what a healthy, full-grown man means by wanting sleep at this hour of the day."

"Ah, if you were in the House representing Ledway you would know."

"I understand. How long is it, by the way, since you did represent Ledway in the House?"

Mr. Earne, whose one thought just then was to get out of the room as quickly as possible, did not at first quite catch the meaning of this, and answered absently,

"About three years."

"I shouldn't have thought it was quite so long," said Mr. Brail reflectively; "if you had said three weeks now."

"At any rate, if I am to go there this afternoon, I must leave you now."

"Then you may as well take Miss Maulden home with you. She is going too, and means to walk; it is only a step out of your way."

No suggestion could possibly have been more awkward. Mr. Earne could not possibly have excused himself, and Serena dared not offer to stay behind, lest she should betray him. They submitted, said good-bye, and left the room together.

Mr. Earne's brougham was waiting for him outside. The coachman had, like his master, an unmistakable out-all-night expression, but did not look nearly so wan and dissipated.

If Mr. Earne had looked jaded and disreputable in the softened light of Mr. Brail's room, he looked and felt infinitely more so as he stood on the steps in the relentlessly clear full morning light. He stood a moment, looking at Serena's sweet, bright face, so fresh and healthy, seeming all the fairer for the brilliant sunlight playing on it—longing to apologise for the necessity of leaving her in the street after promising to see her home—wondering miserably if any apology would be adequate to the outrage of even appearing before her in such a state; then he did what was probably the very best thing under the circumstances; he simply raised his hat without speaking, bolted down the steps into his brougham, and shut himself in out of sight.

Serena walked home by herself, thinking that this silent penitence had been very eloquent, half resolved already to undertake the task her old friend had set her.

CHAPTER II.

THE WORKING OF IT.

"I DON'T think it is exactly—manly," said Serena.

"Oh, but it is, my dear. A diffident but hopeful lover would naturally confide the ups and downs of his courtship to a friend, and I want to hear the latest. Did you go to the picture gallery?"

"Yes," said Serena. "I went when you told me. I was there when he came."

"What did you say?"

"I said I had come to see the pictures because you had told me so much about them, and he said he had come because you asked him to make notes for your benefit. We made notes together. I think when you hear them you will find they are a good deal more my notes than his."

"That is very good."

"But I have done better. I made him take a very long walk with me. I don't know how, but I did it. I think I looked surprised when he was *not* going to do so."

"That's the best way. Don't seem as if you wanted, but as if you expected attention. I believe the strongest and most long-lived instinct in that kind of a man is the habit of courtesy, the instinct of a gentleman ; people will do things involuntarily, and without noticing what they are doing—which they certainly would not do if asked. I remember the case of a man, who, in a fit of anger, but accidentally, had almost killed his dearest friend— indeed, for some time it could not be known whether he had not quite killed him. Well, this man was in a wild state of remorse and horror, and would not leave his friend's bedside. He would take neither food, nor drink, nor rest. His wife begged him with tears to take rest for her sake. His mother tried to force him to eat ; but no—he declared he would neither eat, nor drink, nor rest until he knew if his friend would live. At last he got himself into such a state that the doctor feared for his brain, and said he must be made to sleep somehow, even if it were by means of an opiate. But how to administer the opiate, when he would not even take food ? At last a young lady staying in the house, almost a stranger to the poor fellow, made them disguise the opiate in a cup of coffee, and took it up to him. Being a stranger, of course she did not entreat like his wife and mother ; she simply stood waiting, and he took the cup from her, and drank the coffee mechanically, because it was more natural to him than to keep a lady standing. Yes, there is nothing like trusting to these instincts. You must look as if you expected to be taken home to-day."

"To-day! Is he coming here to-day? He told me Wednesday."

"Yes; I knew he would tell you, so I wrote and asked him to come to-day instead. He will think you came to-day without being asked, and with the idea that he was *not* coming."

"Oh!" exclaimed Serena. "Let us keep our motive in sight; our means are a little vulgar."

"Serena," said the old man eagerly, "you are blushing. I *heard* you blushing. My dear, don't I think of the motive all the time? You have done much good already. Earne is getting more like himself every day, as regards steadiness. I am afraid it is all up with his constituents though. You see they are slow people over there, and they are only just beginning to know all about his falling into evil ways; they won't hear about his pulling himself up—his relapse into virtue—until too late, if you don't manage a little quicker."

"Oh don't! it makes me so ashamed."

"You musn't be ashamed, you must be glad. I am glad, for I begin to be sure my dear friend will be saved."

"I hope indeed he will be," said Serena. "You don't know what it will mean to me, having tried this thing, if I fail. You don't know what it costs me. You know what I have done, how I have gone out of my way to meet him, and when I see him how I study every word I say that it may please him. I think of little pleasant speeches to make him feel at ease and satisfied with himself. I ask him to explain things I know just as well as he does, to keep him amused. Oh! it should be a good motive to excuse all this hypocrisy."

Mr. Brail refrained from the cynical remark that many women did all that and more from entirely selfish motives, because he feared it might make Serena give up her task in disgust if he even suggested a parallel between her and such girls, and because his acute hearing detected something unusual in her voice.

"Serena," he asked presently, "something has happened ?"

"Yes," she said.

"What is it, my dear ?"

"You remember—years ago—my—my—the person I was engaged to. I heard this morning that he is dead."

"Oh, my child, what a blow to you !"

"No, it wasn't a blow at all; that is what is so sad. I don't care at all, not at all, and yet years ago he was so much to me. Is it because I have outgrown feeling that I don't care at all ?"

"Your voice sounds as if you cared."

"Does it ? That is perhaps because I am thinking of years ago and how miserable I was then.

I think I am sorry that I can't be miserable now, I feel so heartless."

"I think I shall let you go home, Serena, before Earne comes," said Mr. Brail suddenly.

Serena went very gladly ; she felt herself to be in an emotional humour, and unfit to play her part that afternoon.   She had been gone about ten minutes when Mr. Earne arrived.

Earne's relapse into virtue, as the old artist called it—preferring that term to reform, which implies that its subject never has been virtuous—was by no means complete, but he looked what he was this afternoon, a fairly good-looking, fairly intelligent, and thoroughly honest man, in indifferent health and indifferent spirits.

He looked round as though he felt the room rather empty, not that he had expected to see Serena, but he had so often seen her there when he did not expect her, that he was disappointed, but he did not say so.   Not seeing her, the next best thing was to talk about her, but he did not know how to begin, so started the subject just then uppermost in his mind.

"How delightfully quiet you are here !" he said ; "if you'd been where I have all the morning, you would appreciate it.   I have just come from the House, in a wretched temper.   I have been listening to stupidities.".

"Is that so unusual ?"

"The stupidities were unusually irritating this

afternoon. Braxton was at the old story: Laws ought to be obeyed simply because they are laws. Why, it makes even a good law seem oppressive to defend it in such a way; how any man who knows history can say such a thing is simply bewildering."

"Have you never noticed," said Mr. Brail, "that as a rule no one does know any history? There is no limit to what the general public doesn't know."

"Well, I don't know much myself, but I know that if one had lived from the Conquest until now, and obeyed all the laws all the time, one would have done some uncommonly queer and foolish thing. I wonder what all those enthusiasts who were so delighted with Braxton's stale fallacies would have said if some one had pointed out that probably eighteen out of every twenty of them were breaking the law at that very moment. They weren't doing anything wrong, and were probably some of them quite respectable, but, if laws should be obeyed simply because they are laws, they were all of them criminals."

"Good gracious, how?" said Mr. Brail. He too would rather have been talking about Serena, but was waiting his chance.

"Because it is illegal to wear any buttons on your trousers but brass buttons with the button maker's name on them, and nobody wears brass buttons now. If I had only known that at the time, I

C

believe I would have come out with it, and reduced the argument to an absurdity, but I didn't; a fellow told me as I was coming here. Shall I give you the notes on the picture now?"

"Yes, please."

Mr. Earne began to read, and the old man listened carefully. Presently he interrupted.

"That's good! that's very true. I didn't know you knew so much about it, Earne."

Earne coloured, for that was one of Serena's thoughts, but he went on reading. Mr. Brail carefully watched for such criticisms as he knew for Serena's, and remarked on all of them. At last Earne had to confess.

"The best part of all this is not mine. I met Miss Maulden at the Gallery, and we made the notes together."

"Oh!" said Mr. Brail.

"You see she knows a good deal about these things. I thought it would make the notes more interesting for you."

"Yes," said Mr. Brail. Then there was a pause, at the end of which Mr. Brail said suddenly,

"Do you think you are quite wise in paying Miss Maulden so much attention?"

"Why, I have not been paying her any; it is she who has been paying me attention."

That was not exactly what Mr. Earne meant, but he was taken by surprise, and the words slipped out before he had time to consider. The moment he heard them, he was as shocked as if the remark had come from someone else. There was a moment's very awkward silence, then Mr. Brail said:

"My dear Stanway, don't you see that you have said something exceedingly shocking?"

"It sounds so, but it is the truth. I should not like to think anything else were the truth. I should be thoroughly ashamed of myself if it were not the truth; besides, I am too grateful for her friendship to risk the loss of it by—presumption. Shall I go on reading?"

He did so until, at one particular criticism of Miss Maulden's, Mr. Brail exclaimed:

"Serena again. Oh!——"

"Why not? if she likes to be my friend who can object?"

"Her father. He wants her to marry."

"Nonsense! Fathers who want their daughters to marry don't leave them alone in a half shut-up town house, and go wandering about the colonies.

"But Serena is going into society again now. She went to Lady Atherton's last dinner."

"She went there to meet me—she is kind enough to like to meet me, and frank enough to say so. Do you think such a woman as Serena Maulden would do so unless she were sure I should not misunderstand her? It is unkind of you, Brail, to disturb our friendship with such suggestions."

"If I don't, someone else will."

"Absurd; she knows me better; why, she knows about Miss Macleod."

"Why, that's all past! you have quite got over that; you know you have."

Mr. Earne had never realised it before, but at that moment he knew that he had; he could talk quite easily now of the young lady who had treated him so ill.

Mr. Brail went on. "And you see Serena, knowing this, might possibly mistake you. I don't say she does, but she was here this afternoon, and left when I said you were coming."

"She probably had another engagement," said Mr. Earne decidedly. "I tell you, if I thought she believed me capable of presuming on her goodness, I would go and tell her at once that she had no cause to fear. We are on such terms—we understand each other so well—that I could easily do that."

"I would if I were you," said Mr. Brail. He was feeling his way. He suspected, from the other's reiteration of his own unworthiness, that he was trying to drag a hint that Serena did not think him so unworthy; but the old man was not going to give such a hint on mere suspicion.

"I would," said Mr. Earne, "if I had only a shadow of an excuse for calling. I have never been in her house before, you know."

"Take her some flowers."

"Oh nonsense! she has plenty of flowers."

"Take her some magazines."

"Take her the 'Ledway Gazette,' with the account of the meeting of my constituents, and a full report of all the pleasant things they said about me," said Earne with a laugh. "Read it to her, and then tell her that the man about whom all these pleasant things are said, and said more or less truly, a man whom one woman did try to love, only she gave up the effort as hopeless, is actually mad enough to want to marry her, because she has shown a little friendliness towards him. No, no, Brail; I prefer to keep her friendship. Let us finish our notes."

And he finished them. And Mr. Brail ; satisfied now that things were going as he wished, found a good deal of amusement in noticing how carefully Mr. Earne left out Serena's opinions.

Presently he left and walked slowly down the street. It was quite true Serena's manner of lovemaking had only had the effect of convincing Mr. Earne that she did not care for him in the least, except as a friend ; but it had made him exceedingly fond of her society, and really grateful for her friendship—almost dependent on her friendship. The idea of losing it through any misconception was really painful. So that while Mr. Brail, according to his habit, which, blind though he was, he had never given up, was busy jotting down the incidents of the afternoon into his diary, Mr. Earne was resolving that he would go and call on Serena, and

he would make asking her advice about his con
stituents the excuse.

Serena Maulden was sitting in a cool corner
of the drawing-room in the big empty house—
Mariana could not have been more alone. The
distinct lines of light that fell through the five
long, narrow windows, seemed to relegate her to
an incident in the background of the big, silent
room. Serena sat dreaming; there was a curious
awakened look in her eyes, as if she had been
brought face to face with herself for the first time
after many years, and was startled. A colonial
paper lay at her feet, in which she had read that
morning of the death of her long-lost lover. On
her return she had found it just where she had left
it when she went out to see Mr. Brail, and she now
sat looking at the paragraph marked with a black
line, as if it were written in a language she had
forgotten.

She heard the door-bell ring, but paid no attention to it; no one of any interest ever came to
the house, except on the rare occasions when her
father and sisters were staying in it. It rang again,
louder this time, she heard the clanging of the wire
downstairs, then a door opened and someone came
up slowly, with the irregular shuffling steps of
a person awakened from an afternoon nap, and
Serena felt a little dreamy sympathy with who-
ever had been aroused to open the door, and was
dropping back into her own thoughts when Mr.
Earne was announced.

She was too astonished to show any astonishment, and received him so quietly that it occurred to Earne he might easily have called without any excuse. However, since he had the excuse with him, he might just as well make use of it, so presently he gave her the paper, saying :

"My friends in Ledway have been discussing me, and I should like you to read what they say."

She looked a little surprised then, but took the paper, and began at the top of the column he pointed out to her. After the first sentence or two she half dropped the paper, asking indignantly :—

"Why should you wish me to read this ?"

"Well, not because it is very pleasant reading for either of us."

"Why then ?"

"I don't quite know, perhaps because I value your friendship so much that I won't have it on false pretences, and I want your advice."

She read to the end ; all Mr. Bolt, the undertaker, and Mr. Gregg, the cheesemerchant, had to say—and they had a great deal too, and most of it was very cutting. Now, Serena was no politician, and had a comfortable feminine idea that when vulgar, uneducated men made disagreeable remarks about a cultured gentleman, whom she herself knew and liked, of course the vulgar, uneducated men were wrong and ought to be ashamed of themselves ; so, when she had finished reading the report of the meeting, she flung down the paper, and exclaimed indignantly :—

"But you can want no advice about that. It would be beneath you to notice such people as these—you will treat them with the contempt they deserve."

"Well, yes," he said slowly, "that would be the best way, if they deserved any contempt to be treated with, but you see they don't and I'm afraid I do."

"But this is not true, or at least not all of it."

"They make things look a little darker than they look to me or to you, but still they have the facts. They say I am insolently indifferent to their interests, that I am idle, and—well, not a teetotaler. All that is true enough."

"But they say worse."

"Yes, they say I have broken my promises. So I have. Yes," as she exclaimed, "that is what it amounts to ; if I had not given them to understand that I should do their work for them as it ought to be done, I should not have been elected. I am all the hard names they call me there."

"Then if that is so, if these plain-spoken critics of yours are in the right, of course the only thing to do is to write and say they shall not have cause to speak so again.

"Ah, but the trouble is they very probably will have cause to say just the same things again. My own idea is to give the whole thing up ; that is what it must come to, with or without my consent, sooner or later. Did you know all this?" with a motion towards the paper, "when you first let me have a little of your friendship?"

"I knew something of it, but it did not seem so bad to me."

"No, it didn't seem so bad to me either at the time, or, if it did, I did not care much. Well, now you see clearer, had you not better throw me over?"

"No."

"Why not? I am no credit to my friends."

"Because I want you to be brave and manly, not childish and weak; because—Mr. Earne, did you ever hear what happened to me eight years ago?"

"Yes," he said gently, "I think most people knew that. You don't mind, do you? There was nothing that was not to your credit."

"I can speak of it now because it is quite past, but that is what made me understand the trouble that made you careless and weak, for I felt it too once."

He laughed, he did not quite know why, but his laugh did not sound in the least out of place as he answered :—

"You did not take to drinking and gambling, however."

"No," she said quietly. "I wonder what would be thought of a *woman* who did."

"You make me feel very acutely what should be thought of a man who did."

"Then don't any more ; you have not any excuse

now. I can't believe you care any more for Miss Macleod; you have only got into the habit of thinking that you do care. Is a woman who breaks her word worth lamenting? Are you not yourself justifying her behaviour and making all her friends say she was right not to trust herself to you? Take up your conscience again, have a reconciliation with your Ledway friends, and, if you can't enjoy what is left of life, at least try to make a good use of it."

"Miss Maulden, it is impossible for me not to see that you care what becomes of me."

"Oh, yes; I care very much."

"Then listen. I am going to do as you say in any case, but you could make it so much easier for me. I have found your friendship wonderfully pleasant. I have never mistaken it, or presumed on it, but I have been profoundly grateful. If you will give me more, I shall value it more. You and I have both failed in love. Let us try what we can do in friendship. Let us marry each other, and see how the thing turns out. If you will do this, it is just possible life may be pleasant to me again, and on my honour I will try to make it pleasant to you. Believe me I will."

"Yes," she said softly, "I believe you will."

If she was acting, circumstances were assisting her acting wonderfully; the news she had read that morning had roused and awakened feelings she did not quite understand; then Mr. Earne's innocent entrance into the net she had been spreading for him touched her with keen self-reproach. Was there not, after all, something of treachery in the plot she and her old friend had laid against this unsuspecting man? She could not look in his face, the colour mounted to her own, her breath came quickly, for a moment she was as literally unable to speak as a girl of eighteen who hears her first offer.

"Well," he said gently, "you believe I will? What else? Serena, shall I have a chance?"

"Should he have a chance?"—by accident he had used just the right words. "Should he have a chance?" Why, was not that all her motive, to give him another chance to succeed in life, and in love, since his first endeavour had been such a a failure? Could anything have been more noble or unselfish than her act as Mr. Brail had set it before her? She had tried to save this man, and she had succeeded; why should she not be glad rather than ashamed? She looked up to answer him, but found he was answered already.

"You would not have kept me waiting so long if the answer had been no," he said, with quiet satisfaction in his voice. "Thank you so much, my dear."

Then he rested both hands on her shoulders for a moment, and stooping down kissed her forehead.

CHAPTER III.

THE RESULT.

SERENA MAULDEN and Stanway Earne were married, and the marriage had been a success, so far, at any rate. When they returned to London in the following spring, there was probably not a more contented couple in all the town and all the suburbs. Serena was completely satisfied with the success of her wooing, and Stanway Earne was on the best possible terms with his wife, himself, and his constituents.

It is true the latter had given him some trouble before he succeeded in appeasing their very just indignation, and he found this the more difficult as he was entirely in the wrong and had no explanation to offer.

When he went down to Ledway he made no excuses, but he did promise amendment, and he took Serena with him, and somehow was forgiven. His past misdemeanours seemed more venial to his constituents when considered together with his pleasant manner when among them. It was shocking indeed that a deputation of influential electors should go by appointment to wait on their representative, and find out that he had forgotten them, and had disappeared no one knew where, and then to discover that he had been one of the highly reprehensible lot who had gone to France to witness the great prize-fight, and had all but got into the hands of the Continental police thereby; but the thing did not sound nearly so bad when he gave a select few of the Ledwayites a graphic description of the fight and flight, and assured them that though, of course, he should not be likely to do such a thing again, it was rather good fun, don't you know.

Perhaps Serena influenced the Ledwayites a little; she was so sweet and so happy. Average mankind is not so selfish as cynics assert, for it is always grateful for the sight of happiness. I remember once being struck by a sudden transformation effected in the expression of two men—hard-up, unemployed workmen—who were standing at the gate of a fine house in the country. They had just been refused help at the door, and were plainly cursing the house and all its inmates. All their worst feelings were uppermost, as they stood there in the deep snow, and they looked about as complete a pair of savage, vindictive brutes as even nineteenth century civilization could produce. Presently two girls came racing down the drive, and one—the taller—fell, shaking out a shower of gold hair all round her.

They both were rosy and happy, and positively screaming with healthy laughter; and as those two savages looked at the fun they began to laugh too, the vindictive glare faded from their eyes—they were humanized simply by looking at other people's happiness.

So it came to pass that the Ledwayites forgave their neglectful, insolent representative, chiefly because he spent his honeymoon among them.

Perhaps some hint of love troubles did reach Mr. Bolt, the undertaker, and Mr. Gregg, the cheese-monger, and induce them to pass lightly over their member's misdeeds, for the Greggs and Bolts of this life worship sentiment.   They would be indignant if accused of it; it would be idle to appeal to them in the name of it, because they like to be thought practical men, with no nonsense about them; but the nonsense, if it is nonsense, is there all the same. And if you appeal to the common sense and let the sentiment do its own appealing, the result is pretty safe.   Mr. Earne had no idea that anyone in Ledway knew anything of his private affairs.   And, indeed, very little was known of them, only that there was some sort of an unhappy love affair.   It was plain this pretty, gracious Mrs. Earne could not have caused it, so she must have shared it.   "Cruel parents, and all that," and, well, lots of steady fellows had been a little wild when their love affairs went wrong.   After all, reports always got more or less exaggerated as they travelled into the county.

It was scarcely worth while asking their member to resign when there would be a general election in a couple of years. By that time they could tell better whether he had really gone to the bad, or only had a temporary attack of dissipation.

Mr. and Mrs. Earne had reached their town house late the night before, and were breakfasting together very late this morning. Stanway Earne would scarcely have been recognised now as the red-eyed, unkempt morning caller of a year ago. He was sunburnt and healthy, and he had the placid, well-cared-for look never seen except in a man married entirely to his content; and in truth a man would have been ill to please who had not been contented with Serena. She was one of those women who always look fresh in the mornings. She looked particularly sweet and bright this morning, Stanway thought as he watched her over the edge of his paper.

Serena looked up. "The Syckells want us to go there to-night before the rush begins. Shall we go?"

"Oh, certainly. We may not have another free evening for so long."

He meant *he* should not, for he had come to town with most virtuous resolutions as to regular attendance at the House; but it didn't occur to him to separate himself even mentally from Serena.

"Let us go, by all means," he went on. "Send them a telegram to say they may expect us. Have you anything else interesting?" he added, rising, "because I must go now."

"Oh, don't hurry, Stan; remember, it is your last day of leisure."

"I wish it were," he said mournfully; "but yesterday was my last day of leisure, unfortunately. I've got to go and see Tinto. You don't call that leisure, do you?"

"Poor Stan!" said Serena. "See what it is to be a politician. I would sooner spend an hour with the dentist than with Mr. Tinto. I might endure his vulgarity, but not his self conceit."

"It is his grammar bewilders me," said Stanway. "I almost go into hysterics wondering what on earth will come next. However, he has his uses, like wasps, and onions, and other trying necessities. What are you going to do this morning?"

"I am going to see Mr. Brail."

"Oh, of course. Dear old Brail!"

Then they both looked at each other, and coloured from different causes. They had neither of them seen Mr. Brail since their marriage, and Mr. Earne thought "But for him I should never have married Serena;" Serena's thought was "I am going to meet my fellow plotter, and I am ashamed to meet him." Then, seeing her husband looking at her expectantly, she echoed:—

"Dear Mr. Brail!"

He looked gratified. "I am glad you say that, my dear. You know what I meant; it is a year to-day since I first saw you in his studio, and but for seeing you there—well, I won't go into that: as it is, I have great reason to be grateful to Brail, and if you are satisfied—why it's all right, isn't it?"

This was rather a lame conclusion for a man somewhat celebrated as an orator; but then people rarely are eloquent in private life. He was standing behind his wife's chair, leaning over her as he spoke, but he could not see her face—he went on meditatively.

"I think, for a mere marriage of friendship, ours is turning out pretty well, dear. I think on the whole we are quite 'chummy.'"

"Yes," said Serena.

He looked disappointed, but she did not see that.

"It is exactly one year since we met that morning at Brail's, Serena. I don't think we either of us regret it."

"No," said Serena.

"I don't know, of course, if I am always all you would wish, Serena, but, if not, you have only to speak."

"I am satisfied."

"You do not ask if I am satisfied."

"Oh, I hope you are."

"Suppose I said I was not."

"Oh!" Serena looked up astonished and frightened. What could he mean? Had he discovered anything? Was he going to tax her with insincerity?

He had certainly no such intention, and utterly mistook her startled expression.

"Never mind, Serena. I am not going to say anything of the sort. I am not going to ask you for anything more than you choose to give. Go and see Mr. Brail, dear, and tell him that we are rather happier than the average of married people, on the whole."

"Come with me," said Serena, for she shrank from seeing Mr. Brail alone, and answering his questions as to the success of her experiment.

"I wish I could; but I shan't get away from Tinto until too late. I will join you if I can, but don't wait for me after five."

He collected his letters from the table and then lounged towards his wife again.

"Well, I must go," but he lingered.

"Goodbye, dear."

It was rather laughable. Here was this middle-aged reformed politician, who had outlived a desperate case of blighted affections and made a marriage of friendship, standing like an awkward young lover in a comedy, beseeching for a word of affection, and his wife too blind to give it to him. And yet if only she had been less troubled at the memory of the part she had played, and the prospect of meeting Mr. Brail, who had induced her to play it, she must have seen what he wanted, for it was plain enough.

After a moment he left in earnest; and she went to put on her bonnet to go to see Mr. Brail.

"If only Mr. Brail did not know," she murmured. "It would not seem so bad if no one knew it but me. And yet I think if Stanway talks to me again, as if it all came by accident, I shall not be able to bear it. How horribly ashamed I feel! and yet it seemed a noble, unselfish action at first, when I began to try to win him for his own sake." Then she remembered the first day on which she felt ashamed was the day when she found, by hearing of the death of her old lover, that the old love was dead, too, and that a new love had begun —that the work she had begun for her friend's sake she must complete for her own. That was why she shrank from meeting her old friend; not because he knew why her work had been undertaken, but because she feared he would know how it had ended for her.

"I can hide it from my husband," she thought; "but I shall not be able to hide it from him. He will know how it is with me from the sound of my voice; he will understand it from what I don't say."

Poor Serena entered Mr. Brail's room trembling. She feared he would ask her point-blank, "Serena, how has it turned out?" and she would have to say, "It has turned out thus. I tried to win Stanway Earle's love from philanthropy, and only gained his friendship; and he only asked me for friendship, and I have given him a great deal more." Her old friend's greeting, however, was utterly different from anything she had expected. As she approached him, he stretched out both his hands eagerly for hers; and when he had found them, he instinctively turned his sightless eyes towards her, and said earnestly :—

"God bless you, Serena!"

"Why? You do not know?" she began.

"I know that you have done a good deed, a noble deed; and you have done it well. You have worked for good in the world; the world is better because of you."

"I am glad," she faltered.

"You have cause. I should have blessed you had the man been a stranger, but he is my dearest friend and you have saved him."

"How do you know?" she asked.

"How do I know? Why, from what the papers say of him; from what I hear from other people who know him. I know it as well as I know that you love him."

"How do you know that?"

He laughed. "From your voice, my dear, even if I had not been holding your hand, and had not felt how your heart leaps when I speak of him. You have your reward, Serena. He is a man well worth saving, is he not?"

"Oh yes, indeed."

"Serena," went on the old man, "when first I spoke of this, I thought only of him—I believe I was fonder of him than of you—but when I saw how bravely and unselfishly you threw all prejudice and fear and—and—femininity aside, and thought only of the good you could do, I began to think of you—and of consequences. And after it was done, and you were married, I was frightened, and saw terrible pictures."

"What did you see?"

"Never mind; they are past now. And now all the pictures I see are very pleasant."

"Show them to me."

"I see, far down a long pathway, stretching from now into the future, the pathway of a sweet and noble life—one life, though it takes two people to live it—I see a true man and a true woman, each doing so well their own share of the work of the world that I cannot tell where the work of one stops, and the other begins. I see well-earned fame, and the content of souls that have done what they could. I see dear children around that man and woman, who love them, and are their pride in this life, and will look after them with reverent eyes when they go up higher. I see yet dearer children—good works, for they are the children of the soul, and will follow them, and be their glory in the life to come."

"It is a beautiful picture," she said.

"Yes; and the most beautiful part of it is that it is true, and I shall see it. Not in a dream-picture as I see it now, but with clear eyes—clearer even than those your youth has, my dear."

"What do you mean?" she asked anxiously. "Surely you are not ill? You frighten me!"

"Ill?" said Mr. Brail, dropping suddenly into a perfectly conventional tone. "Bless my soul, no; but an old man of eighty-two can't reasonably expect to live very much longer, you know. Now tell me all about your travels—about Ledway and Paris and Innsbrück, until I fancy I see them."

They talked all through the afternoon, until at about five Serena saw her old friend was beginning to look tired, so she decided to wait no longer for her husband, and went home.

Things looked much brighter to her after her talk with Mr. Brail, and she was quite in good spirits when she went upstairs to dress to go to the Syckells'. They were, perhaps, the most unconventional people in London. They had a commonplace house in a second-rate part of London; but everyone who had the chance was always glad to go there. It was a house where you might meet anyone; but people never went there for the sake of meeting anyone. They went for the sake of having a good time, and invariably had it. The Syckells knew many distinguished people; but they knew no one simply because he was distinguished. Good companyship—if one may coin a word—was the one essential, but it was an essential. They asked nothing else, but, having that one quality, anyone was welcome—from a bishop to a billiard marker.

Serena was going to dress, because she had the time and the dress; but she knew that if she had been a hospital nurse, with nothing to recommend her but a good heart and good spirits, she might have dropped in on her way home in a white cap and apron, and been as welcome and enjoyed herself just as much as she expected to do clad in the graceful draperies her maid was offering her. If her husband was late, she intended to wait for him. It did not matter being late for dinner at the Syckells'; no one was ever waited for; if a guest came when the soup was cold, he began with the fish; if the fish had disappeared, he began with the *entrées:* indeed, on one occasion, a very eminent judge had come when the dinner was quite over, and had dined heartily and contentedly on cheese and apples.

Serena was just putting the last touch to her toilette when she heard her husband come into his dressing-room.

"Is that you, Stan?" she called. "I am glad you are back in time to come with me. Why did you not join me at Mr. Brail's?"

"I have just come from there."

"Have you? then I wish I had stayed a little longer; but you told me not to wait after five, and he seemed tired, so I left."

Serena turned round when she had finished speaking, and found her husband was standing just behind her.

"I have come to tell you what I have found out."

Without his words she would have known it, only too well.   There was only one thing he could find out that would make such a change in his face.

"How was it?" she said.

"You don't deny it, then?   I was foolish enough to hope you would. Tinto wanted to know at what time Betterton had said certain things to me, and I couldn't remember; but I knew Brail would have it in his diary. He was present when Betterton spoke, and he puts everything in his diary, so I went to Brail—and he gave me the wrong book."

"You should not have read it."

"Oh! don't reproach *me*. I did not read much, but quite enough to see how blind I had been; enough to see that your sweet friendship that I have valued so much was a delusion; to see that when I fancied you liked me—on my honour, Serena, I never fancied more than that—I was deceived completely."

"I meant it well."

"Oh! yes; I know it was very noble of you, very generous, but it is horribly humiliating for me. I had rather you had been a little less noble, and liked me a little more."

" It was not my idea."

This was about the worst thing she could have said ; her husband interrupted her with a bitter exclamation.

" I know ! it was not even that," he said ; "and when the matter was suggested to you, you only acted from the highest philanthropy. I was an interesting case—good material for a reformed character, and you charitably undertook the work of reforming me. Serena, was I so bad as that ? Was my state so hopeless you need have given your whole life to rescue me ? Do you think I would not rather have gone to the devil my own way than have a woman so sacrifice herself ? "

" Don't look at it so," she said. " I was so sorry for you. It seemed so sad your whole life should be wasted."

He turned away with a bitter laugh.

" Why did you not persuade me to join the Blue Ribbon Army, Mrs. Earne ? That would have suited you just as well, and me much better."

" No, Stanway, you must not say that. You will not say that when you have listened to me— when you have thought."

" Oh ! yes. I dare say presently I shall look at it all in a proper light, and be profoundly grateful for your philanthropy ; at present the humiliation is almost more than I can bear."

" My dear, don't say that, let me explain——"

" It can't be explained. I must say it, it is true.

I tell you I would rather have shot myself than have had you do such a thing."

"Stanway," she cried, "has it hurt you so much? Then I wish with all my soul I had never seen you. I did not mean to make you miserable, I meant to help you."

"Oh, I never doubted the exalted nature of your intentions. Let us say no more about it."

He was leaning against the mantelpiece with his back towards her; he did not look up, and spoke with intense bitterness. She stood a moment silent, miserable, and afraid, feeling sure there must be some words that would set right this misunderstanding, but not daring to speak them. What could she say to a man who felt his pride so bitterly outraged? She crossed the room and laid her hand timidly on his arm.

"Stanway, speak to me."

He looked up and noticed her dress.

"You are going out?" he said.

"Yes, to the Syckells'. Have you forgotten? Will you not come?"

"Oh, to the Syckells'! I cannot come now. I must go back to Tinto and tell him the date; but I will join you later. I wouldn't miss seeing them for anything," then, suddenly seeming to remember, "Dear Heaven! to think only this morning it seemed so natural for us to be happy together, and now it is all over!"

"All over! Oh no, Stanway. Of course you are

angry; but you will forgive me. Stan, is it really so bad as that?"

"So bad? Angry? You do not understand. It is something terribly like despair."

And he left her.

Serena was by no means a quickwitted or clever woman, but she was quite clever enough to know when she had been stupid, and as she sat in the carriage, on her way to the Syckells', she began to see that she had been very stupid indeed.

She had plenty of time to think over her interview with her husband, and find out wherein her stupidity had lain. She had said nothing that she ought to have said to her husband, and had understood nothing of what he had said to her, or at all events she had not understood the feeling which had prompted his words. He had spoken of humiliation, was angry to find she had an unselfish and exalted motive in marrying him. "Serena, I wish you had been a little less noble, and liked me a little more." Why had she not told him, in answer to that, that the exalted motive had been lost in very human feeling before ever he asked her to be his wife? Why not? Why, because he had never asked for anything but friendship, and she had given him so much more. And how could she confess that? Would not any woman rather be blamed for giving too little than pitied for giving too much? "I fancied you liked me; on my honour, I never fancied more," he had said. But no: "It is something very like despair," mere disappointed friendship had not spoken in those words, in that voice.   Her husband loved her. Had she not been so blinded and overwhelmed with her own love, she would have seen his in his every look, and word, and tone.   She knew it now, and the knowledge produced at first a sheer delirium of happiness.   She could neither understand it nor realise it, only enjoy it, as only those who have suffered can enjoy.

There is nothing so beautiful as love late in life, when they who thought that all was past, and everything that makes life sweet, dead and cold, are suddenly awakened by a thousand bright voices; when hope rises and cries: "The future is bright, let us enjoy it;" and the heart awakes and cries: "I live yet and can love;" and youth looks them in the face and says: "I am here still, I have never left you, let us go forward together." Surely the rejoicing of those who were desolate is as much sweeter than the inexperienced content of first love, as those rare bright days in the clear warm autumn are better that the cold sentimentality of spring.

Serena was so filled with the delight of loving and being loved, that for a moment she forgot that her husband had parted from her in bitterness.

"It is something very like despair." Well, she would see him soon and make it right; a word, a look, would be enough. She would have gone to him at once, if she had not known she should see him soon. She laughed over the thought of following him to Mr. Tinto's; sending in word " Mrs. Earne wishes to see Mr. Earne," and when her husband came out to her saying, " Excuse me, my dear, I forgot to mention it to you just now; but I am very fond of you," and then sending him back to finish his business with Mr. Tinto. But while she laughed he was suffering; that was a dreadful thought. Now she understood it, it frightened her to think of the dreary hopelessness of his tone, the blank despondency of his face; she remembered suddenly what evil that other disappointment had done him. Thank God, there was no danger now; he would see her so soon, and all would be well. He loved her now far better than ever he had loved Miss Macleod. She remembered how, soon after their marriage, she and her husband had been at a ball, and a young bride had entered with her bridegroom, a pretty, empty-headed looking girl, with a sharp nose and a sharp voice. Earne had started, looked at the girl, then turned and looked at Serena with such an expression of relief and satisfaction, that she had asked who the young bride was.

" Mrs. Galway, thank heaven ! " he had said, and Serena had understood that the girl had been Miss Macleod, and that Stanway had thanked heaven she was not Mrs. Earne. Serena had been pleased even then, but it disturbed her now to think that the disappointment, in regard to this girl, had had such a terrible effect on Stanway. Why, if he loved her better than he had loved Miss Macleod, this disappointment would be even harder to bear. "It is something terribly like despair," the words would recur to her, filling her with foolish, unreasonable fears.

Every story of despairing lovers she had ever read rushed into her mind. She thought of the heart-broken cry of Molière, "Pity me, my friend, my wife does not love me." And Molière had gone to the theatre and played his part, and died. Her husband was gone to play his part. Well, what of that? Men do not die when they **are** disappointed in love nowadays. Yes, but that merely means no one we have known has died as yet. Possibly, all the friends of every despairing lover have said as much until they learned better. Perhaps Molière's heartless wife said something of the sort when her generous, patient husband left her that evening.

The carriage stopped in Galt Street. Serena must go in and wait for her husband in a crowd. At that moment she would certainly have gone to Mr. Tinto's to look for him, in spite of the amusement she had felt when the idea first rose in her mind; only she knew he might already have started to join her, and by going to seek him she might chance to miss him, and so defer their explanation yet longer.

The drawing-room was nearly full when Serena entered; a fair-haired little mite of a woman was holding forth energetically.

"Yes," she was saying, "I pride myself on *not* being frank. Why should we say what we think? It is most likely wrong; if it isn't, it is sure to be misunderstood. No one is so abominably deceptive as your very frank woman. You think she must be true because she is disagreeable; but she isn't. All the while she is saying unpleasant things, and you are congratulating yourself that at any rate you have heard the worst, she is carefully saving up something to be frank about on a future occasion."

"The worst of these very frank people," said someone else, "is that they love frankness so much that they want to have the monopoly of it themselves."

"Yes," said the little fair girl reflectively, "I fancy Miss Saul would not like it if I were to turn round some morning and say to her, 'You are domineering, oppressive, and ill-educated; your nose turns up frightfully, and your clothes never fit you; you are always disagreeable, and on Mondays, when you have been spending the previous day reading sermons and teaching little boys —unhappy little boys—in the Sunday-school, you are worse than an east wind.' She would be quite cross if I said that to her, and yet she is always declaring she likes truth."

"I fancy most people like truth in their neighbours."

"That must be what she means, for if she likes it in herself, Miss Saul is a very self-denying woman."

Serena was beginning to wonder who Miss Saul and the young lady who denounced her so energetically were, when Mrs. Syckell explained.

"Miss Symdon is graduating as a milliner, under Miss Saul of Bond Street. Miss Symdon has an ambition to make money."

"It is very unoriginal, I know," said Miss Symdon, "and rather foolish, for when I get it I shan't know what to do with it, since I never had any before. Mrs. Walter, you have written a great many useful things; can't you write a book to teach us how to spend well?"

"No," said Mrs. Walter; "education will do a great deal, but even education won't do that. People may be taught to dress, they may be taught to ride, or even to write poetry; they may occasionally be taught to cook, but to spend well is the result of heaven-sent genius."

Mr. Syckell came into the room. He said he couldn't come sooner. He had been down at Tramore's theatre. Tramore was going to bring out Alderson's book as a play, and he had been hearing all about it. Mr. Syckell had a carelessly pleasant way of speaking, which gave strangers the idea sometimes that he was only a visitor in his own house. As the company went in to dinner he told them all about the new play, and grew pathetic over poor Alderson's probable sufferings when his well-wrought-out, neatly-balanced book should be hacked in pieces, turned upside down, padded, abridged, and generally vulgarised to make it fit the stage.

Serena looked round the table. Several seats were still unoccupied, that opposite her being destined for Mr. Earne when he should arrive; she had of course explained his absence.

She was in a suppressed fever of excitement, fretting against every minute that passed without his appearance. She made such absent answers to the pleasant-faced, bright young man who had taken her down, that he, concluding philosophically that he bored her, let her alone and held his tongue good-naturedly.

There was the sound of an arrival. Serena waited eagerly. There entered a young clergyman, who had only just come from a weekday service. He said he had brought Mrs. Syckell the list of the people who wanted wine, and had better give it to her at once for fear he forgot it. He walked round and gave it her, and she pencilled an order on the back, and gave it to one of the servants.

Another arrival; again Serena was disappointed. This time the late comer was a lady in superb evening dress, on her way to the first great ball of the season. She brought no news, except that she had sent all her children to bed that afternoon for trying to shave each other with dinner knives.

Another arrival; there were still two chairs vacant, and Serena made up her mind not to expect Stanway until all but one were filled. This late guest was a young barrister, who said pleasantly that he thought people would like him to come late, because then he could bring the evening papers. He offered them to Mrs. Syckell as he spoke, and she began to read aloud all the interesting scraps of news, and everybody discussed them.

"Here is something dreadful," she said, as she came to a paragraph crowded into the end of a column as if the news had reached the newspaper office almost too late to be printed. "Here is an accident."

"An accident! What is it?"

"Someone shot himself in a cab in Oxford Street."

"Poor fellow! I wonder what was the matter," said Mr. Syckell. "It is strange how many people do shoot themselves in cabs nowadays."

"I don't think it at all strange," said Mrs. Walter. "I always feel very like shooting myself when I am in a cab, through dread of the battle there will be when I get out. The more I give the men, the more they storm at me. I always give a great deal too much. I suppose they think that I am a fool and fair game."

Mrs. Walter had a peculiarly emphatic manner of pronouncing the word "fool," as if it were spelt with a *ph;* no mere *f* could convey half so much scorn of her own folly.

Serena looked across at the vacant seat opposite. "It is something terribly like despair." It seemed as if the words were suddenly spoken in her ear. She looked round to see if by any strange chance anyone had uttered them. No, the careless, trivial talk was still going on around her.

"It is natural people should get into the way of putting an end to themselves," the barrister was saying gloomily. "The discomforts so far out-weigh the comforts of modern life all the time, that a trifling extra worry is enough to make one desperate. I'm sure," he went on dismally, "what with the Tories so long in office, and the slamming of doors on the underground rail, and spring getting later every year, and the house rising at twelve so that a man hasn't a decent excuse to offer his wife when he comes home at five, it would take a very little more to make me shoot myself in a cab."

Hark! another arrival? No, it was next door. Still that vacant place before her, and those awful words in her ear. Ah! wheels again? No, they had gone past. Someone was telling an anecdote about Irving.

Wheels again? Yes, and they were stopping at the door this time. No, that was not Stanway's step, yet someone was coming into the room. What did it

mean ? What horrible thing was going to happen ?
The lights raced in mad circles before her eyes, the
voices sounded a far-off murmur in her ear. She
saw the pleasant-faced young man who had taken
her in to dinner looking down at her with that
paternally amused air a man generally assumes
when a woman is doing something he considers
" feminine," and she found that she had seized one
of his hands under the table, and was clutching it
convulsively ; possibly her doing so had prevented
her fainting. She noticed that when the young
man saw her face, he looked startled and hurriedly
poured her out a glass of wine with his disengaged
hand. " Drink it," he said in an undertone, " and
then read the note and you will know."

Serena saw then that a note had been brought
to her. As she took it she heard Mrs. Syckell
speaking :—

" I hope that is not from Mr. Earne to say he
cannot be with us to-night, because we expect to
have some really good singing, though perhaps,
now that the House is sitting, ' he has no time for
such things,' like Count de Lauzen said, when the
lady asked him to marry her."

" I quoted that the other day to Tinto," said
Serena's friend, bending forward to intercept Mrs.
Syckell's view of Serena. " Not about Mr. Earne
and dinner-parties, but nearer to the original. Tinto
was wondering why De Carle had never married,
and I said perhaps because, like Count de Lauzen

he had no time to waste on a wife. "Count Lauzen?" said Tinto. "Count who? Lawson's only a ba'onet, and hasn't any der either."

This young man had never met Mrs. Earne before, though he knew her husband by repute. Of course he had no means whatever of guessing at the contents of the note brought to her, but he saw she was in a state of almost unbearable anxiety, and wished to give her time to read unobserved.

Serena's note was from her maid, and contained only a few hurried blotted words.

"Please, ma'am, could you come home at once? Don't be frightened, ma'am, but something dreadful has happened."

"Don't be frightened." No, Serena was past mere fright when she read that. She felt no tendency to faint now. She rose and quietly offered some conventional explanation to her hostess. She managed in a few words to let Mrs. Syckell see it was absolutely necessary that she should go at once, without making a tragic scene among the company. In a moment someone had brought her wraps. Mr. Syckell himself had rushed to the hall door and whistled wildly for a cab, and in less than five minutes after the receipt of the note Serena was on her way home.

Her own door was open when she reached it; a doctor's carriage was just driving away. Serena sprang from the cab and flew up the steps. The maid was in the hall.

"Tell me the worst at once, Alice."

"Oh, ma'am, it will be a terrible shock for you," gasped the girl.

"Is he dead?"

Serena herself was startled at the sound of her own voice, and the girl burst into tears.

"I see he is," said Serena. "Where is he, Alice?"

"In the library. Oh, ma'am, pray don't go in; it is no sight for you."

Serena almost flung the girl aside, and opened the library door and entered. On the further side of the room someone lay extended on the sofa. There was no mistaking the rigid lines, the ghastly immobility. It was someone dead. Someone, but not her husband, for he was standing beside it. And when she realised this, Serena seemed literally to fling herself across the intervening space until her arms were round Stanway's neck and her head lay on his breast.

"My darling husband! Oh, thank God for this. My love, my love, my love!"

"My poor girl," said Stanway, holding her tenderly, "this will be a great grief to you."

"Nothing is a grief while I have you," she sobbed hysterically. "Oh, my love, my love, my love!"

And he, though such words were of all others the words he wished most to hear, could not in the least understand why she spoke them.

"Do you see what has happened, my child?" he said. "Our dear friend Brail is dead."

"It is he, then?" she said, bewildered. "How did it happen?"

"It seems he discovered his mistake in giving me the wrong book, and afraid I should read, and read too little to understand, he came here. I had not returned. He saw your maid, and she says he seemed troubled. He waited here for me. Alice says he grew more and more agitated as he waited; presently he asked to be helped from the chair to the sofa. Soon after he fell asleep. He was still asleep when I came in, and I found him here; but after a moment or so he woke and started up, crying, 'All is well. My children love each other. I need be anxious no more. I see the best picture of all.' I spoke to him, but he did not answer me. He went on talking of the picture he could see for a little while longer, and then he was silent."

Serena bent down and kissed her dead friend's face without speaking.

"He was a dear friend of both of us, Serena," went on Stanway. "I for one owe him a great deal. It is horribly sad to lose him so suddenly."

"It is horribly sad." Serena hesitated, then gave one more loving, half-penitent kiss to the white cold face, and turned to. her husband. "Stanway, we loved each other very much, he and I," she said; "but I cannot be sad. He would understand, he would forgive me. How can I be sad that it is he, when I thought—I fancied—dear, let me tell you what I thought."

She told her husband of all her foolish fears, and if he smiled over them it was very lovingly.

"The man who shot himself was only a volunteer letting off a blank cartridge," he said. "No one was hurt. And so you thought it was I? Ah, my dear, I can't wonder you thought so, considering the weak way I was bearing a far lighter trouble when first you knew me. No, Serena, I felt miserable indeed to-day when I thought you cared nothing for me; but I should have known and loved you to very little purpose all this time if I were not incapable of such cowardice now. My wife, loving you has been so much to me, that as I came home to-night, I said that even if you did not care for me in the least I must go on loving you and being grateful to you; but when I heard our poor friend murmuring of his pictures I began to hope for something better."

"Ah, yes," said Serena softly. "I always loved his pictures, and this last one is best of all. But, Stanway, now I am sure you care to know, I will tell you—no picture can come near the reality of my love for you."

THE
MAIDEN LOVED OF CLEOMENES.

THE

Maiden Loved of Cleomenes.

M YRTO lay along the broad, hot terrace wall. Thais and Ægle were playing at ball in the orchard down below. They should not have been playing ball; to-day of all days it was least fit that any should think of their own pleasure. But Thais and Ægle did not think; it is so hard for youth to think of a calamity that is only possible, though the terrible "ninth year" had come round again in Athens, and though on the morrow lots would be drawn, and seven youths and seven virgins sail away in the black-sailed ship to death, to-day the sun was bright and the wind warm. Nothing evil *had* happened, and so their hearts *would* grow light in spite of themselves, and they played ball together and laughed over it.

They were not heartless, they had dutifully done their best to be miserable all day, indeed, they had not meant to play, but had been walking up and down sadly enough, speaking of the sorrow of the city; but Thais had picked up a ball by chance, and tossed it idly in her hand, and Ægle had caught it and flung it back to her, and presently they quite forgot what might happen to them, and must happen to some on the morrow.

Myrto, up on the wall, was not thinking how she or either of the two down below might be among the fated seven to-morrow. Her heart was full of a secret she had learned of late of herself, and her colour came and went as she thought over it. She knew that, as the elder of the three, she ought to chide the two down below for their ill-timed play, but she had not heart to do it. Presently the sound of their laughter shot up into the air like the water of a fountain, and she leaned over the wall with a little smile.

"That idle Thais makes my Ægle as thoughtless as herself," she said. "I wonder what their jest is down there?"

"How you laugh, Thais," said Ægle; "do you know, my father calls you 'the swallow,' because he says you are always twittering. I think you are the merriest girl in all Athens. Are you never sad?"

"No," said Thais, flinging the ball high in the air and watching it descend; "no, I've never been sad yet, because I have never had reason. But your father is wrong if he thinks I have no more heart than a swallow. Oh, indeed, I could be sad enough if I had reason. Ægle, I think if Cleomenes did not love me I should die!"

Myrto, up on the wall, started, the colour left her face; with black brows drawn together and hands clenched, she leaned further over the wall; but she was too far off to see how Ægle had turned even paler than she.

"Does Cleomenes love you, Thais?"

"Why, yes, of course he does. Are you blind, or do you think I am? Have you never seen how, when he comes in the evening to talk with Orneus, your father, he always stays in the orchard where you and I are? And if we are not there, Ægle, he will go back to the gate and wait a little, and then come again. I have seen him do so three times in one evening."

"Then why does he not go to your father's house instead of mine?"

Thais laughed lightly.

"Why, Ægle, Cleomenes can't help knowing what everyone else knows, that Alycus is sullen and silent, and cares neither for his daughter nor for talking with his neighbours. Cleomenes knows, besides, that I am more likely to be found with you than in our garden at home."

"And are you sure he comes here because he loves you?"

"Do you doubt it, Ægle? I hope not, for then I shall doubt it too, and that would make me very unhappy—oh, more unhappy than you think. See, here he comes, let us go down the orchard and meet him, and it will seem as if we went that way by chance."

Ægle caught her arm.

"No, no, Thais, do not go! I cannot, after what you have told me."

"Why, come, Ægle, I can't go alone to a man; that would not be pretty of me. Come with me."

"No, no, this is no time for love; think of the sorrow of the city."

"How tiresome you are, Ægle, when I had forgotten it. Besides, our staying here won't help the city."

"No; but our lightness mocks it. Think! seven virgins must sail to Crete to-morrow. Who knows but the lot may fall on you, or me, or Myrto."

"Why, so it may; but then, you know, it may not. Think how many thousand virgins there are in Athens. Remember what Clito the gambler says: 'When the odds are in our favour, we need scarcely fear the gods.' I love so well, that I am sure the goddess of love will keep my hand from drawing the black bean to-morrow. Let us hope that we three may be safe. If the lot falls on any of us three I would rather it were Myrto than you, because I am afraid of her, though she is your sister."

"You must not speak so of Myrto; I love her better than anyone in the world except——"

"Except me, were you going to say! Come, Ægle, dear, pretty Ægle, see how Cleomenes is waiting at the gate; if you love me, come."

And half coaxed, half dragged, Ægle went with Thais down the orchard.

Myrto stood up from the wall. Love and pride and anger, like three opposing winds, all joined in one storm in her face and heart.

"You dare to love Cleomenes! You!" she murmured. "You boast too soon, Thais. You think your love will save you; but what if I set mine against it? What will the gods do then? The stronger love must prevail. You would rather the lot fell on me because you fear me. You may have cause to fear me, for if there is any power in love, or any help with the gods, you shall never see Cleomenes after to-morrow."

So at night, when her father and sister slept, Myrto stole out of the house alone towards the grove of Apollo on the hill behind the temple. None saw her, and she needed no companion. The chief priestess in the temple down below was her friend, and had often talked with her of the sacred rites, so Myrto was well learned in the doings of the gods, and knew the story of at least one maiden who had won the gods to her will even against their own, just as she meant to do now.

She knew how to light the fire, and what sweet herbs to burn, and what words to speak in the invocation. She trembled a little, for the night was dark and the grove very lonely, but she went on steadily with her preparations.

The fire blazed up at the foot of the hill. On the one side stood the temple, silent and black; on the other stretched the sea—black, too, and quiet; only a very faint murmur of it came as far as the sacred grove.

Myrto stood with hands upraised before the flame.

"Kluthi meu o Apollon!"

"Apollo, Lord Apollo, hear my prayer!

"Thou that dealest men doom in pestilence; thou that avertest the plague when men call on thee in supplication, hearken unto me!

"Thou that art called destroyer, and healer, also, by destruction, bring healing to my heart!

"Lord of the silver bow—Loxias, lord of light, send now thine arrow, bearing doom and deliverance!"

There was no answer. The moon rose slowly up behind the temple, silvering the sky, and just touching the top of the trees in the grove. The flame flickered, the white smoke struggled through the thick leaves to reach the moonbeams.

Myrto threw on more herbs, and stretched out her hands again:

"Kluthi meu O Apollon!"

A night-bird cried out sorrowfully in the dark; the wind stirred somewhat, and sent up a shower of little red sparks. They could not pierce the thick hanging leaves as did the smoke, but died out in the air before they reached the moonlight. Was that an omen?

What had been the fate of the maiden of whom the priestess had told her? She had prayed, and the gods had answered, warning her that if she persisted they must grant, but that the granting of her prayers would bring woe and desolation. Should she take this silence of the gods for her answer, and go back to her home, and wait for what the gods would do on the morrow?

What, go back with her prayer ungranted, and see the man she loved wed another, an idle, careless girl, ready to love any man, and only fancying she loved Cleomenes because she was proud, as she might well be, that such a man took any note of her. She could have borne it had it been Ægle he loved, but even though the gods were against her, Thais should never be wed to Cleomenes.

No, indeed! As that other maiden had prevailed, so she would prevail. She would stand there, with hands outstretched, and voice uplifted, until the gods took pity upon her:

"Kluthi meu o Apollon."

In her misery her heart grew even bitterer than before; in that moment it was more for vengeance than for love she longed:

"Apollon, o Apollon."

The moon was high in the sky: it shone over all the hill, though it could not pierce the thick leaves that hung low over the maiden's head; it reached the sea, and turned it all to white fire; there was a murmuring among the trees. Hush! Myrto stood trembling. Did any voice say, "Speak aloud your desire," or was it but fancy?

Her heart burned with shame, her lips trembled with fear at her impious prayer, yet her voice did not falter as she spoke aloud:

"I desire that in the drawing to-morrow the lot may fall upon the maiden loved of Cleomenes."

Scarcely had the words passed her lips when she felt a hand upon her shoulder.

"What, Myrto? Orneus' Myrto, here alone? At such an hour, too? Well, I am glad some fancy made me leave my house to-night and come to the sacred grove."

"Who is it?" asked Myrto, frightened but defiant.

"Come, Myrto, you know me well—Nabis, the magistrate, the very devoted admirer of all beauty, and beautiful Myrto most of all."

"Did you hear what I said?"

"Why, yes, and thought when I heard that you had been wiser to make your prayer to me than to Apollo. Apollo is a god, but I am a magistrate, and have the ordering of the lot drawing to-morrow. Ask of me, Myrto, there is little that I would not do for you."

Myrto trembled. "Do not mock the gods, Nabis, for they have sent you here in answer to my prayer."

"Very likely; I thought I came here because my

wife's relations, and the nurses and physicians were making such a howling in my house, but if I came because the gods sent me here I have no objection; I am quite willing to do anything they want if you want it too, only what is it? I am not a god, but a magistrate, so I must have things made plain to me. 'The maiden loved of Cleomenes' may be plain speaking enough for the gods, but I must know her name. Who is she?"

Myrto trembled. To speak that name was to give up a young life to death. Well—what then? Some must die, and if this girl she hated died, another would be saved; should she mock the gods by shrinking, now they themselves had granted her prayer?

The flame died out at her feet, only the moon shone above now on the grove, and that so dimly through the trees, that she could scarcely, where she stood, see Nabis' coarse, insolent face, but the moon was light enough to wake the birds in the tree-tops, and one of them fell a twittering so loud it sounded just like Thais' laughter in the garden. Myrto spoke:

"Thais, daughter of Alycus."

"Thais, daughter of Alycus! Good! You shall see she will draw a black bean to-morrow; this I will do for you cheerfully. But listen, Myrto, neither gods nor men give their gifts for nothing; to them you give this pretty little sacrifice of herbs and fire. What will you give to me?"

"What can I give?   All the jewels I have would be nothing counted in among the wealth of Nabis the magistrate."

Nabis laughed.   "You speak true, Myrto; I am one of the richest men in the city, and you are only a girl with a few idle trinkets on her wrists and head.   All the same you can give me the most precious thing in Athens, if you will."

"What is that, Nabis?"

"Why, that is as men count it; to one the king-ship, which you cannot give; to another the generalship, which I wouldn't care to take; to another, the treasure chests in the temple; to every-one something different; but to me just dark-eyed Myrto, the most beautiful girl in Athens; give her to me."

"You are mad, Nabis.   Do you dare mock the daughter of Orneus?   You have had a wife these ten years."

"I have had a wife these ten years, but I shall not have one to-morrow.   Did you not understand me that Dœdalia is sick?   She has a deadly fever, the nurses and physicians are with her, but they say she can't live more than a day or two.   Orneus' daughter shall be treated with all honour; give me your promise, none shall know of it but me, and when the time of mourning is passed I will come and ask you of your father."

"Are you a fool, Nabis?" she cried, her anger and scorn swallowing all fear or woman's shame. "Is it likely that she who sought this thing of the gods should wed you? Why should I hate Thais, but that I love Cleomenes? What good should I have of the gods' favour if when he was left free to love me I were wedded to you?"

Nabis laughed mockingly. "You can't have everything, Myrto. If you don't have love, at least you'll have revenge, and that's nearly as sweet to a woman, but if you refuse my offer you'll have neither. Come, is it a bargain?"

"Impious," she cried passionately, "do you dare make bargains with the gods? They have come to my sacrifice and granted my prayer, and sent you here to do their will."

"Maybe so, I'll do it readily enough if you promise; if not I'll go home, and you may wait here and see if they send anyone else."

"How dare you mock so? Do you not fear? I will not promise."

"Very well," and he turned to go.

"Nabis," she called. "Nabis—stay. I am mad with misery. Oh, immortal gods! Is this all you will do for a heart-broken woman? Nabis, have they, like you, no pity for my love, but only for my vengeance?"

"I don't know about the gods," said Nabis, "but as for myself, I am thinking of my own love, don't you see?"

"Suppose I also should draw a black bean to-morrow?"

"You shall not: I'll take care of that."

"But Dœdalia may recover."

"Why then, you have the best of the bargain, and will be free to marry Cleomenes if he will have you."

So this, then, was all the gods would give—a chance of love, a certainty of revenge. What should she do?

How dark the grove had grown, and how cold! How the sea shivered in the moonlight! She drew an inch or two away from Nabis. He grew impatient.

"Well," he said, "what do you say? Will you promise to be my wife, if Dœdalia dies, and shall the lot fall to-morrow on the maiden loved of Cleomenes?"

"Let it fall so; I promise."

And she passed by him out of the grove.

.   .   .   .

The drawing was nearly over. All the seven youths, and six of the virgins, had been marked by the gods for death, and these stood, surrounded by their weeping friends, waiting for the one who was yet to join them. All the friends of those who had not already drawn stood round the market-place, waiting. Orneus was there, with his two pale daughters, and Thais, their friend; Cleomenes was with him, more anxious even than the father, and as pale as the girls.

"Myrto, it is your turn."

Ægle pressed her sister's hand without speaking.

"Courage, Myrto," said Thais, boldly, "I found three gold moths on the very threshold this morning, and you know how good an omen that is. Courage."

Myrto walked steadily forward to the table, where Nabis, as chief magistrate, presided over the drawing; she thrust her hand into the amphora that he held, and drew out the lot. White! There was a murmur of congratulation; unheeding it, she went quickly back to her place.

"A third of the weight is lifted off my heart," said old Orneus, hopefully, and indeed, his face, too, lighted by more than a third of his sorrow, as he knew one daughter safe; but Myrto, looking at Cleomenes, saw that the cloud on his face scarcely lightened at all.

"A third of the weight, I say," Orneus went on; "for this madcap Thais here is as dear as my own, though she is not of my house. Now, girls, it is your turn: the magistrate calls. Go quickly; get it over. Thais, child, you first; you are the elder."

Thais and Ægle walked forward, their arms entwined. Thais, who had been confidently hopeful all day, a little in advance, to take her turn; but at the last moment she shrank back.

"Ægle, I dare not! I dare not!"

"Courage, sweet! you must. We all must. Courage! Think of the three gold moths."

"Ah! but a sparrow ate one before my eyes. I did not tell you that. Oh, Ægle, Ægle, which?"

Myrto smiled. She knew which, for had not the gods heard her prayers? The evil omen was for the maiden loved of Cleomenes.

"Why, Thais, dear Thais; you who have been so brave all day, be brave now, dear. See, Nabis waits."

Nabis winced a little. This girl whom he was cheating to her death was almost as beautiful as Myrto, and it was pitiful seeing her shrink and tremble, to think of the monster crushing and tearing those soft young limbs. She stretched out a slim, shaking hand towards the amphora, where the black token which he had ready for her must meet her touch.

"Oh Ægle! Ægle! I am afraid," she sobbed.

"Poor Thais," said Ægle, "how you tremble! Look, I do not fear; all will come just as the gods ordain. See, I will draw first to give you heart."

And before Nabis had time to understand what she meant to do, she thrust her hand into the amphora and drew out the black bean he had meant for Thais.

A cry of pity and gladness rose in the market-place—of pity for this one fair girl, of gladness because the friends of all whose turn had not come yet knew that their loved ones were safe, for the drawing was over. Thais shrieked and covered her face. Ægle, the black bean in her hand, ran back to her father. Orneus broke into loud lamentation, but his cries were less bitter than the cry that broke from Myrto's very heart, as, looking not at father or sister, but only at Cleomenes, she saw in the sudden despair and horror of his face that though Thais' boast had been vain, and her own impious prayer spoken blindly, yet the gods had indeed granted it, and cast the lot on the maiden loved of Cleomenes.

The drawing over, all went sadly to their own homes, those even whose children were safe, after their one burst of joy, sorrowing for those less favoured of the gods. The seven youths and seven virgins who had drawn death were waiting to-night in the temple for the sailing of the black-sailed ship on the morrow. Myrto wept alone in the garden. Her sister! her own sister! her sweet little Ægle! "I love Myrto best of all the world except ———" Ah, Myrto knew now who it was who had been excepted. Had not the gods known she would have asked no vengeance against sweet Ægle? Had not the gods who heard her wicked prayer heard what she had said—if she had but known it had been to Ægle, she could have given up Cleomenes? The gods were indeed cruel, and grudged happiness to mortals, and were eager to strike, and slow to help.

Nabis had said a word to her after the drawing about holding her to her promise, because the mistake was her fault, for not keeping her sister back, but she knew that neither he nor she had done this thing, but the gods.

As she stood weeping in the garden, old Timæa, the nurse, stopped on the road and spoke to her:

"Well! well! the gods have been in the city to-day, Myrto, bearing life and death, and though we must be grateful for their good, it's no use repining for their evil ; they must do what they will.   From you a sister taken, to Nabis a wife restored—and I wish I could believe that he rejoices for the restored wife as sincerely as you weep for the lost sister."

Myrto looked up absently.

"What are you talking about, Timæa?" she said.

"What all are talking about in the city, for it's a happier thing to speak of than the fate of all these poor girls and boys.   When Nabis, the magistrate, went home after the drawing, he found Dœdalia miraculously cured of her fever.

And as Myrto turned, wondering, from Timæa, she saw Cleomenes beside her.

"Poor Myrto!" he said.

"No, poor Cleomenes, rather," she answered ; " I saw your face in the market-place to-day."

"Did you know she was promised to me, Myrto ? I had loved her.   I spoke to Orneus when I was here last night.   Myrto, she was to have been my wife."

She could not speak, but wept, and he, feeling tender towards her for the tears' sake, waited silent awhile.

"I have been with your father," he said at last.

"How does he bear it?"

"Why, Myrto, better than you or I can.   He is old, he thinks most of the loss to his house ; but you and I only think of Ægle."

Brave as he was, his voice broke at the name, and his lips trembled.   It was more than Myrto could bear.

"I will go in to Orneus," she said.

"No ;" he laid hold of her arm to stay her.   "No, Myrto, do not go in, you will not find him."

"Where is he, then ?"

"Gone down to Alycus' house with Thais.   Dear Myrto, it will grieve you to hear, but you must know.   Orneus thinks of his house, and fearing his children will fail altogether, he will marry again himself.   He has gone now to ask Alycus for his daughter."

"But Thais loves—I mean, what does she say to it ?"

"Why, I think she is pleased ; it seemed to flatter her pride that so great a man as Orneus should wish to marry her.   He will comfort her for the loss of her playmate, and she him for the loss of his daughter."

"Ah yes, they may comfort each other," cried Myrto bitterly ; "but who will comfort you and me, Cleomenes ?"

"Why, I must speak of that, too, Myrto, for your sake ; for if I leave it to your father he will speak more roughly than I.   He is determined, since one daughter is lost, that the other must marry."

"The other ?   Me ?   To whom would he give me ?"

What did it mean ?   Dœdalia was recovered,

Nabis could not have asked for her. Why did Cleomenes look at her so kindly but so shamefaced? "To whom?—to whom?" she repeated.

"Why, Myrto, to me; he loves me, and would be glad if our houses were joined—he is very eager for our marriage."

"And you, Cleomenes?"

"I, dear Myrto? Can you not see how sweet it would be to me if Ægle's sister would love me and share my sorrow, and let me comfort her in hers! but it is not of myself I think. I only spoke to you now because your father is absolutely determined you should marry, and I thought for Ægle's sake you might rather come to me than another. But for this I would not have troubled you with talk of marriage, with the tears still in your eyes, and tears still in your heart that shall not find your eyes for many days yet. What shall I say to Orneus? If you will not wed me he will give you to someone else; another husband might chide you for your grief, Myrto, but I shall not."

"Have you any heart to wed, Cleomenes?"

"No, Myrto, no more than you; but as your father reminded me, it is a man's duty to the State to marry, and it is your duty to your father, and since each must marry it is best we marry each other. We two loved Ægle so well, we can surely love each other when this sorrow is past; for who sorrows for ever? Do you for these reasons consent?"

So she had complained of the gods too soon ; she had all she had asked—her rival gone, she free from her promise, and Cleomenes willing to wed her. Willing ! why he desired to wed her, though it was but in tenderness he had spoken to-night to forestall her father's despotic order.   Though at her word, in respect for her grief, he would refuse to wed her, yet if she consented he would receive her consent as a boon and be grateful ; grateful and faithful too, for that was his nature, and some day, when Ægle was forgotten, perhaps even loving——

"I consent, Cleomenes."

He did not kiss her nor take her hand, because he respected her grief so deeply ; it was a very cold plighting.

They sat silent ; the sun set, and a cold wind came through the trees ; Myrto shivered a little ; presently she moved away from him a step or two. After a moment he followed her silently.

Walking slowly and silently, they reached the crown of the hill ; it was quite dark among the trees.

"It is cold here and damp, Myrto," said Cleomenes ; "why do you come ?"

"See, Cleomenes, there is a seat here ; let us rest. We can see the sea from this hill ; I saw it last night. The moon will soon turn it to silver."

"I do not like to look upon it, Myrto.   I should fancy I saw already the black-sailed ship floating out of the bay across it.   See, that is the way it will take—but no, do not look, rather turn your eyes away."

"Cleomenes, do you think you will love me when we are married?"

"Yes, Myrto, for the sake of your love to Ægle, and because I am grateful to you for the comfort you will bring."

"Will you remember always that I wished to give you comfort?"

"Yes, indeed, have I not said so?"

"See, Cleomenes, where that light is in the temple. I wonder does Ægle sleep beside it?"

She felt him start at the name, but he did not speak.

"Sweet, brave Ægle; who knows but for her kindness in drawing first to give courage to her friend she would be with you now instead of me?"

"The gods have chosen."

"True, they are strong and cruel, and we reeds in their hands to bend or break, yet they let us choose our fate sometimes. Think, Cleomenes, Ægle weeps beside that light; would you not wish to see her once again?"

"Myrto, if it might be."

"It might; the chief priestess is my friend, she would trust Ægle to me for an hour if I persuaded her hard, I think."

"Would you indeed try?"

He spoke eagerly but uncertainly, longing for her to do him this favour, but ashamed to take it from his promised wife.

"Yes, Cleomenes, I will try."

She rose, made a step or two, then paused : "You must think, Cleomenes, that such a thing as this is hard for a woman to do. Will you remember in the days that are coming that what I did this night I did unasked of my own free will ? "

Without waiting for any answer, she turned and went down the hill ; he watched her as she went, impatiently, for the mere hope of seeing Ægle again had filled his heart with fire, yet with her kindness still in his mind he noticed as he never had before, how very black her hair shone in the white moonlight, and how proud and stately was her step. He thought of her very kindly as he waited, and told himself a man must needs love so noble a wife, but he wearied for Ægle's coming. It grew very late : the night was half-spent ; had Myrto failed to persuade the priestess ? No, or she would have returned alone ; if she did return alone he would love her, even for having made the attempt, but surely Ægle would come. How late it grew—could she have missed the way ?

At last, when his impatience had almost grown to despair, Ægle stood before him.

When the first sweet despair of such a meeting was past, and they had time to speak a little, Ægle told how hard Myrto had laboured to persuade the priestess, and how she must stay but a short while. "Myrto is resting in the temple," she said, "she will come to call me when I must go back."

Then, with arms about each other's neck, they

spoke long together, sorrowfully but lovingly. She told him what joy it had been to her to love him secretly this long time, and of the pain that had gone through her heart that morning in the garden at Thais' words, and she laughed a little in triumph to think that after all she, and not Thais, was loved, then rebuked herself for unkindness to her friend.

And he told her how light-hearted Thais had been quickly comforted, and how she was to marry Orneus, and he told her he had never loved any but her, even when she was a child he had loved her, and had waited patiently for the time to come when he might ask her in marriage, only for this end. Then she fell to weeping, but her tears were not altogether bitter, for she wept them on his breast, with his arms fast about her.

At last, wearied with the long day's sorrow, child-like she cried herself asleep, and he held her so very quietly, lest she should wake to her sorrow again before she must needs, that he presently fell asleep too.

Down below in the temple the priestess came and spoke to Myrto. "Do you not see how near day it is, Myrto? It is more than time you went to bring back your sister. Hasten, or it will be full day before she is here, and it would be great dishonour to the whole city if one of the seven virgins failed us when the ship sails."

Myrto rose from her seat without speaking, and went out of the temple. There on the west side of the hill it was very dark still, but when she reached the grove a faint streak of pale yellow touched the furthest edge of the sea, the black of the sky was turning purple.

There on the bench, locked in each other's arms, the lovers slept. There were no tears in Ægle's eyes now, her smile was as happy as a child's, and her face was flushed as if she dreamt of her lover's kisses, but Cleomenes, sleeping seemed to feel the nearness of sorrow, for his face was furrowed, and he groaned once or twice as he slept.

Myrto stood looking upon them, knowing what she would do, and resolute to do it. Only they slept, so instead of the tearful parting she would have taken, she would only go away quietly to her death, and they see her no more: see her no more, and so only knowing her deed and not her reasons, all their lives would be burdened with the memory of what would seem too great a sacrifice if they did not know it was an expiation. It was just that they should know the truth. Drawing her tablet from her bosom, she began to write:

"The sorrowful Myrto to Cleomenes and Ægle, and to Orneus, their father."

She began to weep from very pity of her own story.

"The sorrowful Myrto!" indeed. She pressed her hands to her breast to still her sobs, lest they should waken the sleepers. Oh, it was hard, very hard, to lay bare all the tale of her unsought love, her impious prayers, and her shameful promise to Nabis, for the eyes of these two happy lovers to read; it was hard, but true and brave now at the last, she spared herself in nothing, but wrote down all, and laid the tablet at their feet.

The lovers never stirred, the sun came slowly across the sea; there was time yet for one kind word at parting if the lovers woke, but they did not wake. Well, it was best so, she would leave them now; how would they think of her when they woke?

Stooping, she raised the tablet again, and added a few more words: "I pray you for the love of the gods, think kindly of me; read what I have written for truth's sake, and then forget my crime, and only remember my sorrow; or, if you must needs remember the crime, remember, also, I conjure you, happy brother and sister, I did it for love's sake."

So she laid the tablet on the ground again, and now she must leave them indeed, and go to her death.

"Ægle, Ægle! we loved each other so, and I never meant to 'wrong you. I would not have wronged you for the world, sweet sister Ægle; do not wake; but speak my name sleeping."

But Ægle lay quiet as a happy child; her smiling pink lips never moved.

"Cleomenes, you would have loved me, oh, indeed, you would have loved me in time. Think of me a little when you are happy with her, Cleomenes, think of me kindly. Farewell, Cleomenes, farewell!"

The sun flooded all the sea with gold, and drowned the east side of the hill with light; the other side was in shadow still, and it was almost dark by the temple, but Myrto knew the time was short. "Farewell, farewell. If I might have had but one kind word from you! Ægle, sweet little sister, remember me by this. Would you wake if I kissed you— Cleomenes, would you wake?"

Then, remembering the cold betrothal, and how even when he had taken her by the hand to thank her from his heart for her offer to bring Ægle, his lips had not so much as drawn nearer to her, the woman's soul cried out that now—now, at the very last, for love and death's sake, her lips should have so much delight, though Cleomenes slept and never knew it, so she drew near and bent over his sleeping face.

"Cleomenes, love, farewell, farewell!"

But he stirred, and murmured in his sleep; and, fearful lest she should wake him, she drew back quickly. It was her name that he murmured. And Myrto smiled as she drew her veil about her, and ran down the hill into the shadow.

Hours after, when the sun was high in heaven, Ægle awoke from her long, heavy slumber, and, affrighted, called out to her lover.

"Cleomenes, Cleomenes, awake—look, look, the sun is high; it is broad day, and I should have been back in the temple. Why has not Myrto come for me? Cleomenes, why has not Myrto come? What does it mean?"

"Strange," said Cleomenes, bewildered still, and scarcely awake. "I thought she had been here. I was sleeping heavily and dreaming; yet, though I could not wake myself, through my sleep and my dreams I thought I knew she was here."

Then why did she not wake me and take me back to the temple? No, no, Cleomenes, she has not been here; she has lost her way in the night, and could not find us, or she thought, perhaps, we had fled faithlessly, and betrayed her. O Myrto, Myrto!"

"I know she stood here," Cleomenes answered. "She stood here weeping; I saw her drop something in your bosom, and I tried to wake and speak, but could not."

"In my bosom," said Ægle. "Why, yes, indeed. See, Cleomenes, her kerchief—she has indeed been here. And, oh, the gods! look! look! Cleomenes, there sails the black ship far out on the sea. I understand now, my noble sister has gone in my place! Ah, why did she do it? How shall I bear it? Myrto, dear Myrto!"

"It seems indeed, she has done so," said Cleomenes gravely, "and see, Ægle, here is a tablet left at our feet to tell us why."

He took the tablet and began to read:

"From the sorrowful Myrto to Cleomenes and to Ægle, and to Orneus their father."

"Yes, yes," cried Ægle eagerly, "what next, what next? Read, Cleomenes, read."

"Why, I cannot, Ægle ; what should come next is blurred ; the sun has been shining on the wax, the writing is lost."

So it was. Apollo, pitying at last the woman's grief, had showered his warm shafts on the tablet, till they melted the wax, and effaced the record of Myrto's fault.

But not the message of her love, for Cleomenes looked at the writing closer.

"See, Ægle, a few words are still clear at the end. I can almost read them. Yes, yes, I see what they are ; listen !" and he read :

"I did it for love's sake."

Weeping softly, her head still resting on her lover's breast, Ægle drew his hand that held the tablet towards her, and kissed the words tenderly. Cleomenes still stood, troubled and wondering. What were those last words Myrto had spoken before she left him ? It seemed as if the memory of that kiss, that through his dream had come so near his lips, yet missed him, were still in the air. He turned round sharply ; Ægle turned with him.

And they saw the black sail drop down behind the glittering sea.

AN UNNOTICED INCIDENT.

An Unnoticed Incident.

———◆———

CHAPTER I.

A WIFE.

A BITTER wind was driving the sleet fiercely round all the corners, as Mrs. Railton, turning out of Hammersmith Road, neared her own door. She was carrying a heavy parcel by the string; her feet were wet, her eyes aching with the cold, and the sleet, which had found the weak place between her bonnet and her cloak, would probably give her a very bad sore throat; but Mrs. Railton was not thinking of these things. She was thinking of summer—one summer fifteen years ago. How bright it had been, and how hot, everywhere but in the wood, and even there the breezes had been faint and warm. What wonderful shapes the great patches of light that fell through the outspread arms of the great tall trees had taken! What glorious colours had lain among the shadows where the foxgloves and thunder-flowers grew in crowds. Ah, that was a pleasant place, and she had stood there leaning against a willow by the river, looking up eagerly into the handsome, eager face bent down to her.

She almost heard her own voice saying:

"I am not fit to be your wife, Donald. I am so stupid and so ignorant."

And in answer he had told her that clever men always hated clever women, and that her sweet childishness, her naïveté, and simplicity were dearer to him than all the wisdom in the world. Yes, those were pleasant times, and that was the happiest day of all her life, clouded perhaps by a passing fear as she listened to this new lover that "Cousin Dennis" might be disappointed; but the cloud only stayed for a moment, for she did not know then how to be unhappy—nothing had ever happened in her life to teach her the way.

Now all these memories were very pleasant; but they were very unwise. It would have been much wiser of Mrs. Railton to think of the washing-bills and the water rate, or to plan how she might best disguise the long tear in Kate's ulster and make it down to fit Jane; but then, as her lover had joyously pointed out long ago, Mrs. Railton was not wise, but rather the reverse, and unfortunately, the qualities which had been so charming to the lover then, only served to irritate the husband now.

Indeed, it is an unfortunate fact that the men who are the readiest to dispense with cleverness in a pretty girl of seventeen, are the most intolerant of the want of it in a wife of thirty, and never hesitate to tell the poor wife—if they happen to meet with a clever girl who will notice them at all—what a relief it is to talk to a woman with a mind!

This is puzzling, and bewilders the poor wives as to what is really expected of them, for it is not everyone who can regulate herself to the perfect medium : that is, be clever enough to appreciate her husband, but not clever enough to criticise him.

Mrs. Railton rang the bell, and waited while the one harassed-looking servant came up from the dim regions below. She heard the noise of the family in the sitting-room at tea. They were in the habit of opening the door to each other, but it did not occur to them to disturb themselves for their mother. Father never did, and why should they? When Mrs. Railton entered the room, Kate said, "Are you wet?" and Jack said, "Are you hungry?" and they went back to their previous subject of noisy discussion.

There are few things give one a more chilling shock than to come home and find one's place filled, one's wants forgotten. It gives one a foretaste of death, faint, perhaps, but unpleasant. Mrs. Railton looked round the table; no one made way for her. Her husband looked up and said crossly:

"I wish you would try not to be late, Lisa, it sets such a bad example to the children."

Kate rose from the head of the table, saying :

"You will have to send for more tea, this is finished." But neither of them seemed to expect an answer, so Mrs. Railton gave none. She rang the bell, and while the harassed servant was bringing up some tepid tea and a semi-raw chop, pulled off her damp gloves, and found that her finger, which had been passed under the string of the parcel of books, was bruised and cut. She had not noticed this while her hands were so cold, but it began to ache and smart as she held her fingers to the fire.

Mr. Railton went to his arm-chair and lit his pipe ; the children went to the other end of the room and discussed their lessons in undertones. Mrs. Railton attacked her comfortless tea. She was cold, and tired, and miserable, and longed foolishly for a little sympathy; so she asked for some.

"I have hurt my finger," she said.

"How did you do it?" said Jane, looking up from her books ; but then, Jane, was always glad of an excuse to look up from her books, so her sympathy did not count for much.

"I was carrying these books for your father, and I never noticed that the string was cutting my finger because my hand was so cold. Those law books are so heavy."

"You should have changed to another finger," said Kate, practically. She was a handsome, clever girl, very like her father, and was certainly far too wise ever to hurt herself doing things for other people.

"Did you say you hurt yourself? Where are the books, by the way?" said Mr. Railton. "There! Oh, thank you." Then, as he looked at them, he added, fretfully: "They are all wrong ; just as I might have expected."

"Are they really wrong, Donald? Oh, what a pity! I was so afraid of making mistakes that I gave the list you wrote out to the librarian, and those are what he gave me. I am so sorry they are wrong."

"I might have expected it," muttered Mr. Railton crossly. "I wish I had gone myself, here's a whole evening wasted. I came home early on purpose to read. I might just as well have been at the office."

"I am so sorry," repeated poor little Lisa.

"So am I," he said sharply, and leaned moodily against the mantel-piece.

"Are you quite sure they are all wrong, Donald?"

"It is maddening to have a whole evening wasted when I have so few free," said Mr. Railton, testily, ignoring her question. "Since I can't read, I may as well go out. Kate, if you manage to dress in twenty minutes I will take you to see 'Henry VIII.'"

Kate gladly threw aside her books and ran upstairs. Jane began a struggle with George for the French dictionary. Mrs. Railton was not very much disturbed. She was accustomed to be slighted ; but she made a weak protest.

"You should not take her from her lessons, Donald."

"She can look after her lessons herself. She is never behindhand in her work."

"You promised to take me to see 'Henry VIII,' and I think——"

"Oh, that's what you mean, is it, by your anxiety about her lessons? Paul, go upstairs and tell your sister to come back to her books. Your mother wishes to go instead of her."

Paul, a chubby, stolid boy of eight or nine—considered the clever one of the family because he made least noise—only opened his mouth, and waited. He smelt satire in his father's tone, and knew he should not have to go on that errand. Poor Lisa felt more miserable than ever. She knew she was being wronged, but she did not know how to state her case.

"I am much too tired to go out," she said.

"Then you needn't spoil my pleasure by making me think you want to," snapped her husband.

Lisa knew he was not at all likely to disturb his enjoyment by any thoughts of her ; but she was not sharp enough to say so, which was just as well, perhaps. Kate called at that instant to know if she might borrow her mother's opal brooch, and Lisa went upstairs to get it for her, and see that she was well wrapped up.

Presently a cab was whistled for, and the father and daughter drove off.

The Railtons were in tolerably easy circumstances. The children went to good schools, and Mr. Railton could have afforded a better house and more servants, if he had not preferred to save in that respect, and spend the money in ways pleasanter to himself. If anyone had suggested that he ought to make life pleasanter to his wife, he would have regarded such an idea as sentimental nonsense, declaring that he was an exceedingly good husband, and that Lisa had everything she wanted ; and as for house-work, that was a woman's duty. "Want pleasure, indeed ! A married woman ought not to want pleasure ; she ought to stand aside at her age, and let her girls have the pleasure." A precept, by the way, he did not dream of applying to himself.

Donald Railton was a lawyer—getting on fast, and meaning to get on much faster, but, unfortunately, in his progress he had left the eager lover, who assured sweet little Lisa Grey that her simplicity was the very quality for which he had chosen her, so far in the past, that now he had not even patience left for his jaded, spiritless wife, and much preferred the company of his sharp, animated daughter, who could understand him, and who never looked in his eyes with the reproachful wistfulness that sometimes made his wife's face so irritating.

Mrs. Railton had been sitting by the fire about half-an-hour, engaged in making a new petticoat for Kate, when the door-bell rang, and the harassed maid appeared, announcing:

"A gentleman, ma'am; shall I show him in the drawing-room, or in here?"

"Why, in here, of course," said a cheery voice; and next a tall, bearded, bronzed stranger stood in the doorway.

"Cousin Dennis!"

"Cousin Lisa!"

"Oh, Dennis; how tall you have grown!"

"My faith, Lisa; how thin you are!"

And these greetings over, Cousin Dennis West came forward into the room and spoke to the children, seated himself by the fire, and plunged into conversation.

"Tell me all about everything," he began. "How is Railton? Getting on like a house on fire, I suppose; and in a fair way to become Attorney-General, or something equally distinguished. And how are you, Lisa? You are as pretty as ever. May a cousin say that, now you are a dignified matron? I remember fifteen years ago, you refused to sing duets with me for a week, because I said something like that."

Mrs. Railton was not so pretty as she was fifteen years ago; but if Cousin Dennis thought so, it was pleasant that he should say so in that frank, brotherly tone. She asked what he had been doing all these years.

"Making money, dear; such a lot of money, quite a fortune; and I have come to London to invest it. I am going to ask your husband's advice—he knows everything; he always did know everything. I say, Lisa, do you remember Larne Woods fifteen years ago?"

Did she not? Had she not been thinking of it only that evening; though this dear kind Cousin Dennis had held but a small place in her thoughts.

"What a cub I was then!" went on Cousin Dennis. "And how Railton sat on me, and you, too! You despised me because I was three months younger than you, and very properly too. What an exhibition I made of myself, and how you must have laughed at me!"

"I was so young," said Lisa, for she could not deny having joined in Railton's laughter, though in her heart she had been sorry for the poor, petulant boy, who had taken her engagement to the handsome young lawyer so bitterly to heart.

"Yes," laughed Dennis, "I was three months your junior; that was the offence. You called it a year—you remember—because your seventeenth birthday had passed a week before, and I was still only sixteen. But it is only three months, you know. Well, Lisa, you will be glad to hear that I very soon got over my disappointment; indeed, I have had a good many more since. I say, Lisa, now I look at you again, you don't look half so well as I thought you did. Have you been ill?"

It was true. Now the flush of pleasure and surprise had faded from her face, she looked, as she generally did, ill and worn. She murmured something about being overtired this afternoon.

"You are indeed, I can see," he said, "and you are sitting in an uncomfortable chair all this while." He jumped up and looked round the room. "Here, youngster, move out of that," and disturbing the stolid Paul from a low folding chair, he brought it round to the fire, installed Lisa in it, brought her a footstool and a screen, and then, reseating himself, went on pouring out reminiscences, while Paul stood by with his mouth wider open than ever.

Their talk was all about the time long ago when Lisa was a merry, light-hearted girl, the happiest in a happy home, with father, mother, brothers, and cousin all ready to pet her; when life seemed one long holiday, and time was reckoned by skating expeditions, and hay-making, and nut-gathering.

"And the piano, Lisa—the dear old piano. Do you remember our duets on it? Can you still play the barrel-organ with three notes missing? Do you remember 'Garyowen'?—our own arrangement when I played the air down in the bass, and we made it sound so gloriously inebriated? Could you play it now?"

"Let's go upstairs and try. Is there a fire, children?"

Jane said: "No, there wasn't."

"Never mind, we can light it," said Dennis. "Do you remember when we got up at four o'clock to gather mushrooms, and never went further than the kitchen fire? We lighted it, you know, to cook some breakfast, and then sat, making toast and drinking coffee, until we fell asleep, and didn't wake until cook came downstairs to make the regular breakfast."

They had gone upstairs while he was speaking, and Lisa lit the gas, and was about to put a match to the fire which, after the manner of second-rate households, was ready laid, and seemed about as little likely to burn up as a fire laid some four days before it is required invariably is.

Cousin Dennis said: "Allow me," and took the matches from her, noticing the hurt finger as he did so.

"Why, what is this, Lisa?"

"Nothing, nothing at all."

"Yes it is.   How have you hurt it?"

"It is nothing; only carrying heavy books."

"Why, Lisa, since when have you taken to reading 'heavy books'? And were you so anxious to improve your mind that you damaged your fingers?"

It impressed the children vaguely that their mother did not say the books were not for herself;

they would have said so in a moment, and got all the sympathy they could. Their mother got sympathy enough, however, even on the misunderstanding that she had hurt herself in her own service. Cousin Dennis despatched Paul for vaseline, and Jane for an old handkerchief, and made just as much fuss over mother's little ailment as mother would have made over one of them. This astonished the children completely; and all the evening, while Lisa talked and laughed like a girl over old by-gone jokes, and by-gone scrapes and adventures, they crowded round her to listen, with a respect for her unknown before.

Mr. Railton, when told of Dennis West's arrival, remembered him faintly as a forward boy, whom he had very properly put down, but did not take enough interest in him to be pleased, or displeased at his reappearance until he heard about the money. Then he was pleased, naturally, the mere novelty of the thing was delightful. In these hard times we are so much likelier to meet with people who want to raise money than to invest it. So he made Dennis welcome to his house, and gave him a good deal of very useful advice. Dennis had a good deal of money, as he had said, but it was scattered at random over the globe. Wherever, in his restless life he had happened to acquire money, he had invested it on the spot in concerns good, bad, or indifferent. The good investments Mr. Railton advised him to leave alone. The bad were to be called in at once— even at a loss—but the indifferent were to be dealt with cautiously. The most extensive among the latter were in Mergui, and it was settled between the two men, that West should go out again presently, fortified by a great deal of advice from Railton to dispose of them satisfactorily. Meanwhile, Dennis West went often to the little house in Upton Street, and the oftener he went, the less he liked it. Not only because on a nearer acquaintance he found Donald Railton to be narrow-minded, selfish, and contradictious, but because he saw Lisa incessantly worried and slighted, and had to see it in silence.

CHAPTER II.

A FRIEND.

"Oh, I had once a true love,
Now I have—a very ill-tempered husband.
And I had three braw brithers, but I hae tint them
    a'.
My father and my mither sleep in the mould this
    day.
I sit me lane—in the midst of a house full of very
    unattractive and intractable children."

DENNIS hummed this very free adaptation of one of Lisa's songs one afternoon in March, as he walked towards Upton Street. Poor Lisa! The words just expressed her case. Once she had everything, now she had nothing. The husband of her youth had failed her utterly, and her children were so painfully like their father. Poor Lisa! Once the spoiled darling of a happy home, now the tired drudge of an inconsiderate household. He could not see how she could possibly have any pleasure in living.

Dennis West was a naturally light-hearted man, who had never realised that the greater part of mankind have no pleasure in living. He thought of his poor little cousin's troubles as something exceptionally sad and terrible; to-day, as he neared Lisa's door, he was thinking that, if he did not make haste and get away to Mergui, he must have a big row with Railton, and tell him what he thought of him.

He rang the bell, and waited patiently, for it often took the harassed servant some time to disengage herself from the mysteries below, and put on a clean apron. But presently it dawned on him that as he was not expected, the family might be out. Then it occurred to him that on such a fine afternoon everybody might be in the garden. So he walked round the end of the road, and up the lane at the back, counting the shabby brown doors until he found the right number. The door stood open, showing the narrow strip of damp garden. Dennis looked eagerly forward to see if anyone was in it, but before he could see, he could hear. Only the old story—something had gone wrong, and Lisa was being scolded and sneered at before the children.

"You should have had the children ready in time, and been ready yourself. I won't wait. We have missed one train already. We ought to be there now."

"It is very unkind of you to leave me behind."

"It is your own fault. You had better come on by the next train."

"I will not come alone on a visit, and let every-one see how my husband treats me."

Dennis moved away quickly, partly because he knew what bitter words would follow Lisa's indignant speech, and he did not want to hear them, and partly because he knew the shortest way to the railway station was through the back garden, and he did not wish Railton to see him. He might change his mind, and stop at home, and Dennis did not want that now; he wanted to see Lisa, and cheer her a little if he could. He heard the noisy party troop out, he gave them time to turn the corner, and then he entered at the gate. Lisa stood alone in the garden, the early spring light falling round her seeming to mock the big tears on her face.

Her surroundings were not poetic. The little trim rows of cabbage plants and carrots were sprouting feebly on each side of her. The damp mould of the path, sprinkled stingily with a few ungainly pebbles, looked dull and squalid in the afternoon light; in the background, the harassed servant was languidly shaking a duster out of a bedroom window.

Dennis stood in the doorway looking at Lisa. She had on a big print apron, and it was rather dirty; her hair was untidy, her face tired and flushed, very possibly it was somewhat dirty too. But Dennis West did not see all this—he only saw that, standing there, she suddenly put up her hands to her face and broke into helpless, hopeless tears ; then she turned without seeing him, and went into the house, her head bent, her shoulders shaking with sobs.

And seeing this, Dennis was filled with an over-mastering pity. It was true—as he had taken pains to make her understand—he had quite overcome his old boyish love; but he had not forgotten his friendship for the playmate of his childhood, nor his gratitude to her father and brothers—who had been brothers and a father to him—and for friendship sake, and for gratitude, he would do what he could for Lisa now.

He could not do much ; he could not change her husband into an ideal lover; he could not reform her children, nor plant groves of trees all down Upton Street to improve the prospect ; but he could at least go there oftener than ever to cheer her up. He could talk over old times with her, play over old tunes, keep her husband in good temper, and prevent the children plaguing her at least one evening every week ; and he would do so, even if he had to let the Mergui property go to ruin.

He waited about half-an-hour, and then went round to the front of the house and asked for Lisa. He found her patient and sweet as ever, ready with conventional excuses for her husband's absence, and not a sign of anger or discontent on her face, and finding this, his pity and veneration for her grew all the deeper.

Dennis not being married, there is no means of judging what sort of a husband he would have made himself; but there is no limit to one man's indignation when another man neglects his wife. Indeed, however indifferent a man may be towards his wife, one wonders that, if only for policy, he does not conceal it before other men. The sight of a slighted wife invariably raises all that is noble and chivalrous in an onlooker, and a friendship, founded on chivalrous devotion on one side and gratitude on the other, is about the most dangerous friendship that can exist between a married woman and a man not her husband. It assails her on her weakest and most womanly side—the need of protection. It enlists all his best qualities on the side of wrong-doing, until while she thinks she is only grateful, and he only means to be generous, they drift past all help.

When Dennis thought everything over that night, and in his own mind reaffirmed his unspoken resolution to remain in London for the sake of rendering poor little Lisa's life as bearable as possible, he went to sleep with an easy mind, utterly unconscious that any practical person would have told him none but a fool or a knave would have made such a resolution.

CHAPTER III.

A MOTHER.

THE spring, and summer, and autumn had passed monotonously, but more pleasantly, to Lisa than any time had been since the first few months of her marriage. It was winter now again, just a year since Dennis West had dropped so unexpectedly into her life, and in all that year his friendship had never failed her. He was away just now—something had gone wrong with his business affairs, and he had been spending the past week or two in looking after them.

It was cold, bright, frosty weather now, and Mr. Railton, who was certainly a hard-working man, was taking advantage of one of his rare holidays to give his family a day's skating. The children were all mustered in the hall, and Mr. Railton was looking over to see if they were in every respect fit to go out with him.

" Lisa, look at that child's gloves."

Lisa looked. Paul's stumpy fingers showed

five dirty red marbles at the ends of each glove.

" Put on your best gloves to-day, Paul ! "

" I haven't got any best."

" Yes, dear. I bought you a pair a fortnight ago. Where are they ? "

So she had; but Jane had been surreptitiously wearing them to school every day, and this was the result.

" I haven't any but these," Paul said stolidly, with a hazy notion that either he or Jane was in for a row, and that it had better be he, because Jane was only a girl.

" You naughty boy, you know I bought you a new pair.   Where are they ? "

" There, there, don't scold the poor child and spoil his day," said Mr. Railton fretfully. " I really think you might try to have the children decently dressed when I am going to take them out."

So it was mother who was in for the row after all. Well, mother was always in rows; still it seemed rough on mother that she should be scolded because they had not obeyed her. Paul got just a glimmering insight into the evils of responsibility without authority at that moment.

When they reached Regent's Park, they found all the ponds were bearing, and a good many skaters were on each. The frost had not lasted long, and the Humane Society were in full force with all its ghastly apparatus. The sight of the ropes and ladders startled Lisa, and she timidly suggested that they should enquire which was the shallowest pond. The shallowest pond, however, proved to be also the most crowded; so Mr. Railton decided to try that by which they stood, where only a few skaters were disporting themselves, and, ten minutes later, they were all on the ice.

There is nothing like violent exercise for driving away low spirits, and there is no exercise more delightful than skating—so slight a motion of the muscles sends this heavy body, which drags so wearily on foot, flying lightly along, the fresh wind blowing in one's face, the warm blood dancing and racing through all one's veins, in the intense enjoyment of motion, without the fatigue of motion. We rise to the level of a bird when skating, only, Mercury-like, our wings are on our feet.

Before long Mrs. Railton was enjoying herself thoroughly, and Mr. Railton laughing happily with the children. The children skated well, and did not need to be dragged about, which was fortunate, for Lisa would certainly have done most of the dragging; and, as it was, she was in a fair way to spend the afternoon very pleasantly indeed.

She watched her tall, stylish daughter skating about with her father, and thought how well they looked together. So did the younger ones as they dashed about in couples.

Lisa was the odd one of the party; but it did not occur to her to let that trouble her. Fresh people kept coming on the ice. She enjoyed watching almost as much as skating.

Presently, as she stood at the further end of the pond, her husband and children came skating towards her; they stopped as they neared her, and for a few moments they all stood in a group watching the rest of the skaters. A stalwart couple, both about six feet high, came skating clumsily, but happily, along, wavered, clutched wildly at each other, and fell. A few good-natured people rushed forward to assist them, when there was heard a resonant crack, and a long white line shot across the entire width of the pond. There was a chorus of "Ohs" —half laughter and half fear—and a general stampede for the shore. Mr. Railton was one of the first to move; but in a second he recollected, stopped, hesitated, then seized Kate in one hand, Paul in the other, and made for the bank, calling to the others to come on.

Lisa stood breathless. She had seen the pause, the consideration—" Which shall I save "—and that she had been left; and the sight took away all desire and power to move.

Next second, two strong arms seized her shoulders, and she was hurled, rather than drawn, into safety.

Everyone stood silent on the bank, waiting to see the water bubble up through the crack; but they did not see it. The ice looked as strong and as safe as ever, and presently people began to realise this and to feel foolish.

Lisa heard a low, jolly laugh, and, looking up at her rescuer, saw a big, black-bearded man, who took off his hat and began apologising for his unnecessary roughness.

"No danger whatever; the ice is just settling down, I suppose you knew that, and so didn't move. I thought you were too frightened to stir, and so I just shot you off. I hope I didn't hurt you; but I saw you were quite alone, and it took the disgrace off my own flight to rescue somebody."

He laughed again, and started on the ice once more, followed by several others.

"I say, he thought mother was alone!" said Paul. "If the ice had broken, and you hadn't got drowned, I should have been glad he was there, wouldn't you, father?"

No one seemed disposed to follow Paul into these abstract speculations. Mr. Railton changed the subject abruptly, saying:

"Nonsense, don't let a little crack like that frighten you. Come along."

Mr. Railton was, perhaps, just a little ashamed of himself, and that made his tone all the harsher.

"I do not care to come."

"You can't stand about all alone in the cold. If you won't skate you had better go home."

"I will go. Tell the children I am tired. I need not ask you to take care of them."

"I am sorry you are tired. Mind and take a good rest when you get home," and he skated after the children round the corner, leaving her on the bank.

A sudden turn brought her bearded rescuer to her. He saw her struggling with her skates, and stopped. A look of good-natured remorse overspread his handsome kindly face, as he noticed her colourless lips and trembling hands.

"Going? Let me take your skates off, and let me apologise again. I can see I frightened you, though the crack didn't. Perhaps I hurt you ; but we never have any ice in Ireland, so I don't understand it, and I really thought there was danger, and, as you were alone—— Pray do not be angry with me."

He changed his sentence because he saw that for some reason his words troubled her, and supposed she resented his addressing her a second time ; though, indeed, the veriest prude living could not have taken offence at his frank, impersonal manner, Lisa felt a sudden rush of emotion to think a stranger should care to deprecate her anger.

"Indeed, I am not angry. I am very much obliged to you."

"Then I hurt you. You are looking as white as a ghost."

"No, not at all ; indeed no, only I am tired, and

not very well, so I am going home. Thank you," as he gave her her skates neatly strapped together; and she made an effort to look strong and independent as she walked up the low, steep bank.

"One moment," he said.

She turned.

"I'm waiting for my wife," he said, "but she won't scold me if she has to wait for me when I tell her what I have been doing. You must let me see you home, or at least to the station."

"Oh, thank you; no, it is not in the least necessary."

"Not in the least," said another voice. "It seems I am come just in time to be of use, Lisa."

"Oh, Dennis, I am so glad to see you back again."

"That's all right, then," said the stranger cheerfully. "I can leave you with an easy conscience."

"Thank you, very much," said Lisa.

The stranger waited just a second, because, if the new-comer were the lady's brother or husband, it was only natural that he would want to make some acknowledgment of his attention to her; and such was the frank cheerfulness of his manner that Dennis found himself instinctively murmuring some indistinct courtesy. Then he and Lisa walked towards the gate in silence.

Presently Lisa said:

"Don't you think he must be rather a nice husband?"

“Who?”

“Why, he; the gentleman who took off my skates.   I was tired, and wanted to go home, and couldn’t manage the straps.”

“Didn’t Donald know you wanted to go home?”

“Yes, of course I didn’t go without telling him; but he was at the other side of the pond.   I dare say he did not know I was going just at that moment.”

Poor Lisa! between her sense of discomfort at what she took for a rebuke in Dennis’s tone, and her dislike of explaining her husband’s neglect, she spoke very lamely.

But she was mistaken.   The disapproval was not for her, for Dennis had reached the bridge a moment before the ice cracked, and had seen and understood the whole incident.

“I don’t think it was exactly proper,” she said, “but he only meant to be kind, because he saw, I mean thought, I was alone.”

“You were alone,” Dennis said abruptly.   “When I am not with you, you are always alone.   When will the others come back?”

“Oh, not till late; they are going to a little party after the skating.   I had forgotten that.”

And she remembered that no one had recalled it to her mind, or asked if she would not join them when she was rested.

They walked on in silence to the Marylebone Road; as they crossed it, a sickly, hideous column of smoke rushed up through one of those ventilators so peculiarly suggestive of a private entrance to the infernal regions.

"Oh, dear," she said, taking a deep breath of the clear, frosty air, "we have to go down among that to get home."

"We are not going home," said Dennis quietly, "we are going somewhere—anywhere, it does not matter ; a picture gallery will do."

"I think I should like it," said Lisa, hesitating. "I am not wanted at home; the children will not be back until the evening ; and Donald will be quite late ; and a picture gallery will be such a pleasant change."

"That's it," said Dennis shortly. "It is time you had a change."

They walked on through the hard, dry streets until they reached the gallery; but when they entered it, Dennis led her past all the pictures to a quiet seat, and signed to her to sit down. She looked up surprised.

"We came here to talk," he said shortly. "Lisa, I was on the bridge just now, and I saw all that happened."

She saw something in his face she did not understand.

"Then—it is no use pretending any more ? " she said.

"No, it is no use pretending any more. Lisa, all this year you have been pretending not to be wretched, and I have been pretending to believe you.   But I have known all the while how things were."

"Yes," she said. "I pretended to be satisfied when I thought you believed me ; but that is no use now.   It is often like that—nearly always when you are not here."

When he was not there.   And he had come to tell her that he must go away for good.   That was the news he had brought back from his three weeks of inspection.   His losses had been so great, his affairs had become so involved, that nothing but his own presence could stave off ruin.   He must tell her that he must leave her—almost at once—leave her now she had grown used to his friendship—leave her without a friend in the world, to bear her troubles alone.

Poor Lisa ! poor glad-hearted, bright-souled Lisa, had she been made only for this ?—to wear out her life as the despised drudge of a man who has tired of her ?   And must the man who loved her as a child, and loved her now with a new love, so much more deep and tender than the old, leave her to bear the burden alone ?

No, never.   She had as good a right to love and happiness as any woman in the world.   Why should she live this long, slow death, when he could give her far better things ?

"You want to tell me something," she said.   " Is it—is it that you are going sooner than you thought ? "

"I am going at once."

She watched him with parted lips, waiting, perhaps guessing what was coming, for his voice had no sound of farewell in it.

"Lisa," he went on, "when I first came back I tried in my blundering way to show you that my childish love for my pretty tyrannical cousin was past, outgrown."

"Yes, I understood; if it had not been so, you would not have come."

"I would not, Lisa. I came back to be your friend, and I stayed to be your friend, and I saw your sweetness, and your patience, and your suffering. And now I love you ten thousand times more than ever you were loved in your beautiful youth."

"Oh, my beautiful youth!" It was a cry of bitter regret for good things hopelessly past.

"There is no woman on earth more to be pitied than you. Your youth is gone, your beauty is gone, and you have nothing instead of them."

"Why do you tell me?" she said wearily. "Do I not know?"

"Lisa," he went on, "some women have to bear poverty, and bear it because their husbands love them. Some have to bear neglect, but their lives are passed in ease, and they do not mind it; others who have neither love nor comfort have pride and pleasure in their children. What have you? No one loves you but I, why should you not love me?

No one wants you but I, why may I not have you ?
Lisa, I swear to you that if your husband loved you,
I should not ; if there had been any hope in your
life, I should have been content to have passed out
of it in silence ; but you know as well as I do, that
the shock once over, no one will even miss you.
Remember what happened just now."

It was true, she knew it.   If she had died that
day, she knew how little difference it would have
made in her home.

" Your husband, whom you trusted in your youth,
fails you now.   Can you deny it ? "

" No."

" And to which of your children can you turn,
saying : 'This one at least will be the comfort
of my age ? ' "

" To none of them."

" Lisa, you will come with me to-night, to
Mergui ? "

They stood facing each other, a few feet apart.
There was no passion in their voices or their eyes.
She only waited while he spoke with quiet con-
viction.

" You have no idea what it will be like," he said.
" Instead of your life here with its endless slights
and loveless patience, instead of the burden which
has worn your poor weak hands and bruised your
dear true heart, you will have rest, and perpetual
summer, and soft airs, and endless love and tenderness."

" I will come."

The words struck him painfully. He thought that was because the practical every day view of it all hurt him, and her consent brought him to it.

"We will go to-night," he said. "I have had news which makes it absolutely necessary that I should go at once. If you come with me, Donald will never guess where we are. He will not think I have gone to Mergui, because I have so often spoken of going there. He will think that was only a blind."

" I dare say."

The train starts at 11.30. Will you come to my rooms? That will be better than your going to the station. Stations are so crowded. I should not like you to be in a crowded station at night."

" I will come."

"He—Donald, I mean—will not be back until late, you say? The steamer will have started before he finds out you are gone."

" I suppose so."

"Till to-night, then. We must part now. I have things to arrange. Do not be late."

" Good-bye."

"Good-bye, Lisa, my love. I will make you so happy."

"I hope so, I think so; and I should like to be happy before I die, and no one wants me here."

She rose as she spoke, and he put her into a cab at the door.

"Do not be later than eleven," he said.

"No."

She did not look up as the cab drove off, she sat as in a dream. So it was all over—the long, bitter, joyless struggle—she was going to be happy at last. One person in the world wanted her, she would go to him, and her place here would simply close up. No one would miss her; no one would even be surprised; whatever she did had always been displeasing. She had tried so hard to be good all these years, and what was the use? She would try to be happy now, that would be much easier.

The harassed servant showed no surprise as she re-entered, only inquiring if, since she had come home, she would clean the plate as she usually did on Wednesday afternoons. Lisa said "Yes," and put on her apron to begin, laughing softly to herself as she polished the best teapot and the not very numerous spoons and forks, to think she should never do such work again, for she was to be a drudge no longer, but a happy woman, loving and loved.

The time passed quickly, she was astonished to find how late it was. When the children returned from the party they were tired, which was fortunate, for it made them inclined to go to bed, and they went on her suggestion without any opposition. The eldest girl had stayed with her father. Lisa was annoyed and distressed, for grown-up parties and late hours were even more harmful for Kate than for most young girls. Then she recollected that nothing Kate did need concern her now. There was positive rest in the thought already.

Poor Lisa! A strong-minded, high-spirited woman would have known better, would have known the road she was taking had never yet proved the road to happiness. A wise woman would have seen the weakness of Dennis's arguments, would have understood better what she was doing. But poor Lisa was not wise, and had no strength of mind or will. Donald Railton had chosen a fool, and, having married her, had blunted her faculties, and dulled the little intelligence she had by neglect and harshness; she had got into the way of doing what she was told when it was unpleasant, now she would do what she was told when it seemed very, very pleasant indeed. Who among her family could reproach her? Who of them all deserved that she should still sacrifice herself to them?

It took her very little time to make her few preparations. It was a quarter to eleven as she stood on the landing ready. The door into the boys' bedroom stood open, the gas was still full on; mechanically she entered to turn it down. The youngest boy was in his crib; she passed by him almost carelessly. Paul lay asleep with one hand grasping a crumpled paper. There was a certain beauty in his stolid, chubby face after all. His mouth, too, looked actually pretty when it was shut.

"How I would have loved my children if they had cared about it," she murmured, standing over Paul's bed, and half-ashamed of offering unsought tenderness, she stooped and kissed him.

"Mother," he started awake suddenly, rubbing his eyes with his left hand. "Yes, it's mother," and he held out the crumpled paper towards her.

"What is this, Paul?" and unfolding it she saw two squashed macaroons in the last stage of dampness and stickiness.

"They're from the party. You didn't go, and I thought you'd like some."

"Paul, did you think of me at the party?"

"Yes, lots. I've been thinking a long time. I've been thinking——"

"What have you been thinking?"

"You're always doing things for us, and nobody is good to you but Dennis, and he's going away and there won't be anybody; so I am going to be always like Dennis to you."

Young as he was he was thoroughly English, and looked more ashamed of his good impulse than if he had been caught stealing jam. His mother was looking at him in eager wonder. He went on, mumbling his words, scarlet-faced, and rubbing his eyes with both hands now both were free.

"Father's always scolding you, and we bother you, and Tommy Brent's mother isn't half as nice as you; but they are all good to her, and we're horrid; but I won't be any more."

"My son, my son!" she cried, "do you understand what you say? You will not forget to-morrow? You are so young, you cannot understand."

She flung herself on her knees by the bed, gazing with piteous eagerness into his half-awakened face, and, as she looked, the soul of the child stood up in his eyes, and she knew it was no childish whim, but the beginning of a great joy for her.

He put his warm arms round her neck, and fell asleep there.

Ten minutes to eleven. She would soon be with him, and everything was ready. Dennis paced up and down his room in a fever of impatience, more miserable than ever he had been in his life. He had triumphed; that is, he had succeeded in making the woman he loved, less than she might have been. She was worse, not better, for knowing him. He had persuaded her to do wrong in the hope that, together, they might find happiness; and his misery had begun already. Lisa! the patient, gentle saint, he had worshipped. He had made her no longer a saint. He, who had meant to be her best friend, was now her worst enemy. He had loved her for her purity, her sweet patience, and endurance. What if he ceased to love her now he himself had destroyed those qualities! It would not astonish him. Nothing would astonish him that he found himself doing now. He had thought himself honourable and upright, and he was neither. He had thought himself a true friend, and he was none. Now, when he thought himself a faithful lover, how could he tell that he was not mistaken? He felt himself so false and contemptible that no further discovery of baseness in himself would have surprised him. It grieved him to think that Lisa had trusted herself to one so contemptible. He remembered how he had always believed that such actions as his ended in wretchedness. He believed even more certainly now. How could he trust his good intentions to Lisa, when those other good intentions had broken down? How could he be sure of his love when his friendship was such a miserable failure?

The clock struck eleven. He started. She would be with him in a minute, and there would be no going back. The thing was done already.

Just then he heard the door open. He groaned and hid his face. He had realised his own fall already; now he knew that she, too, was in the mire with him.

"Telegram, sir."

It was the landlady who entered. Dennis took the envelope, and read the contents.

"Do not wait for me. I cannot come. Paul loves me. You have taught him to love me. Good-bye."

He bent eagerly over the few half-illegible words. Slowly their full meaning reached him; then he raised his face, and said, "Thank God," quite firmly and quietly.

Donald Railton is getting on in the world. He is in a fair way to become Attorney-General, and is more satisfied with himself than ever; he never knew what an escape he had had that December evening, which was as well, for he was incapable of under-standing the story had he heard it. He noticed that his wife grew daily brighter and stronger, and prob-ably thought she was growing wiser as she grew older. The other children noticed that Paul never contradicted mother now; and, moreover, that he punched Will's head for so doing, and when his mother rebuked him for it, listened quietly, and said he would not do so again.

All this roused their astonishment at first, and then their respect. They grew to understand that mother had a champion now, and that the clever one of the family. They grew to see how eagerly their mother waited for Paul when he was out, and what a pleasure it was to Paul to tell all his news to her at the end of every day, until at last, they, too, began to change their manners, and see all the sweetness and loveableness of their mother's character. Kate, indeed, will always be her father's daughter, and none of them will ever be to Lisa what Paul is; he is her strength and her joy, something daily to thank God for. Satisfied with his love, her husband's bitter words grieve her no longer. Now that she has a defence against them he has naturally ceased to speak them, and any advance he makes she meets much more than half-way. She has resolutely turned her back on the past, and life grows daily brighter and brighter.

But perhaps years hence, since Cousin Dennis will probably soon be married to the Consul's daughter at Mergui, whose name had been so often in his letters lately, perhaps, when Paul speaks to her of some woman he loves, and whose love he has won, she will, in warning, tell him of that dangerous moment in her life, and show him a crushed cracker paper holding two crumbling macaroons.

MISS MAY'S GUEST.

MISS MAY'S GUEST.

BEATRICE MAY had been to a very "smart" party, and was walking home to save her cab fare. She went to all the smart parties because she was a very charming girl, well-known in artistic society for her crisp, vivacious little landscapes, and in the society that, though not artistic in itself, loves art and artists, for her pretty face and good spirits; and she was walking home to save a cab fare, because she had very little money to spare, and moreover, to-night she had broken out into the wild extravagance of a cold roast chicken for tea, and wanted to make up for it. It was far too cold to think of going home by bus.

It was the coldest evening of all the cold winter; the wind seemed armed with steel knives; it rushed spitefully through the streets, and flinging itself furiously on the few hardy enough to brave it, found out all the weak places in their armour in a trice. It seized the man with the weak heart, and, shrieking,

K

"This is the way I kill such as you," froze up what little vitality he had. It shook the man of feeble chest, and crying, "Here is your vulnerable spot—here, here," sent him home to cough and gasp for breath all through the long night. It set its sharp teeth in among the nerves of the weakly, the famished, and the old, and danced devil's dances there.

It didn't hurt Beatrice May to any great extent, for she was a vigorous, healthy young girl, with a constitution that defied even such a wind as this; but it lashed her insteps and her ankles, crept down between her hair and the collar of her coat, raced up her cuffs at the wrists, and froze her hands dead in her muff.

So when she reached the baked-potato man, who has his stand at the corner of the Earl's Court Road, she stopped to buy two-pennyworth of hot potatoes, with the double purpose of warming her hands on them, and supplementing the chicken.

She stood blinking at the red glare of the stove, noticing how cold her very eyes felt as the lids closed over them; and while the potato man, frozen into indifference even of this unusually interesting customer, was languidly choosing out such potatoes as were sufficiently cooked, she noticed a man standing near looking at the fire.

He was too far off to be feeling any warmth from it; he was only staring at it in a dull, apathetic way, as if finding some slight relief in the mere sight of it.   He seemed absolutely in the very last stage of cold and hunger.   He was standing with his long thin arms wound round his body as far as they would go, his lank black hair falling round his grey, attenuated face, which was thrust deep down into the collar of his tightly-buttoned ragged coat ; he had the air of holding himself together for want of something to lean against.   He looked at Beatrice with the same dull, apathetic stare as he looked at the fire— both were too far off to affect him personally, but still, merely as a reminder that such things yet were in the world, were faintly pleasant to him.   Looking at him, Beatrice felt that if she had not worked hard for the food she carried, and every article of the warm clothing she wore, she should have been ashamed of possessing them.

She had been putting the potatoes into her muff mechanically—they would not all go in, the potato-man was offering her the last two.

"No, they don't matter—I have enough ; give those to our poor friend there."

The man looked up : looked at her, not at mere life and beauty in the abstract, a part of the moving background of that little spot of red light, the little show of warmth that was his last comfort, but at her personally, as a woman who required an answer of him.

"Thank you.   There is really no reason why you should give me potatoes, but I am very much obliged to you."

The voice was quiet and well-bred, past all question the voice of a gentleman—her equal—her brother. No, not her brother because her equal, but because of the pain and pride in his face; because, young and healthy, and happy as she was, she felt their common kinship to sorrow and death; because, had a persistent run of ill-luck made her as poor as he, had the cold pierced her through, and hunger pinched her features as sharp as his, she too would have found the humiliation of taking careless alms from a stranger more bitter even than cold or hunger. She looked at him and shivered, feeling for the moment all he felt; then she spoke again, impulsively, as was her habit.

"See here, my friend, you want more than a couple of potatoes; I shall be so pleased if you will come home to tea with me. You will—will you not?"

"You are very good. I will come with pleasure."

The words were spoken with the mechanical courtesy of habit. The man was far too cold to feel any emotion, even the feeble emotion of surprise, but he made an effort, unknotted his arms, raised his head—as it were, gathered his bones together and shook them into place—and moved with Beatrice down the street.

The potato man stared after the two amazed; he thought it all very improper, unless, indeed, this well-dressed lady was a little mad.

But Beatrice was not mad, only very Bohemian; perhaps in her heart she was a little amazed at herself, but she was far too kindly-natured to insult her guest by showing embarrassment now her invitation had been accepted. She went on talking pleasant commonplace till they reached her rooms, well aware that her companion was not listening, but to avoid an awkward silence. She carefully refrained from asking him any questions. Indeed, his faculties were so benumbed with the cold that he could not have answered her if she had questioned him. He only knew that he had ceased dying of cold for the moment, that a sweet and gracious woman was talking to him, and that presently he should have something to eat ; but the instinct of good manners helped him every now and then to say something vaguely appropriate in answer to her.

"I live here," she said, as they reached a neat little block of red flats. "I am on the third floor. We will go up slowly, because I can see you are ill."

"Thank you."

They went up the dimly-lighted stairs very slowly indeed. Beatrice would have liked to have offered him her arm, but, seeing him half stretch his hand to pull himself up by the banisters, and then draw it back and take the wall side to leave the banisters for her, she refrained. When they reached the third floor, and Beatrice opened her door, a little rush of warm air came out into the cold to welcome them. The man gave a low, half-articulate murmur of pleasure, and bent forward eagerly towards it, as if his unsteady feet could not take him into the warmth quick enough ; they went in together.

"Ah, my gas stove is such a comfort to me," she said. "Before I had it, I used to have to light my fire when I came in, in the evenings, and sometimes it would not light ; now this is all I have to do."

Threading her way across the almost dark room, she knelt down in front of the stove and turned on the gas to the full, so that the little blue line of light along the bottom bar sprang up in yellow flame, and curling among the asbestos globes in the grate turned them all bright red. He could see his way now, and, with the same little murmur of pleasure, made a few steps towards the fire, blinking his deep-set eyes, and pushing the lank black hair off his face with both hands.

"Take this chair," said Beatrice, when he reached her. "Wheel it a little nearer the fire, please, and then it won't be in my way while I am getting tea ready. I call it tea because it would be absurd to call a meal dinner when I get it ready myself, and we don't dress for it ; but I always want something substantial at this hour, and if you would rather consider it dinner, we can have claret instead of coffee —only I am afraid it is rather bad claret, and I pride myself on making good coffee. Here is a newspaper, so that I need not feel I am leaving you unentertained, while I ' fly round,' as the Americans say."

All this was said by snatches, and unconsciously rather than deliberately, with an intention of putting her guest at his ease. His mind was still too benumbed to take in the meaning of any separate sentence; but the general effect of them all was warming and soothing, in keeping with the pretty room, the fire and the light, and the prospect of getting something to eat. He felt, rather than understood, that she had invited him to her house in a spirit of comradeship, not of charity, that he was her guest, not her *protegé*—was entertained, not relieved.

He did not read the paper; he watched her over the edge of it, as she moved quickly about the room, and in and out of it. There was not much to do apparently; she had put on a kettle, and brought in a tray of tea things, taken the potatoes out of their dirty skins and put them before the fire to brown, and lit two lamps, one with a cream-coloured shade, and one with a red one, and now, standing before a little glass, just where the two lights met in amber, she pulled off her hat and coat, and passed her hand once or twice through her hair.

Then she drew up a big Japanese screen, to shut off the colder end of the room, and enclose all the warmth and light round the table. Last of all she made the coffee, and at the fragrance of it her guest's frozen faculties began to wake at last.

" I ought to have been helping you all this while," he said.

" You ought if you had not been ill; that is why I did not ask you. Besides, you don't know where anything is kept, so you could not have helped me much.   I say, you know—shall you be shocked if I own to keeping brandy in my rooms? A little brandy and water, before we begin tea, or dinner, or which-ever it is, would be so good for you."

"A dessert spoonful of brandy in a little milk would be better, if I might have that."

It pleased her that her guest should know exactly what he wanted and ask for it without hesitation; she had the brandy and milk ready for him in a couple of seconds, then they drew the table close to the fire, and, being both very hungry, didn't talk much for the next few minutes. It hurt Beatrice at first to see her starved guest struggling to eat like a gentleman, and not like a wolf; it was horrible to see a face as delicate and intellectual as was his, fairly glow with the joy of merely feeding; she felt to the very depth of her heart the agony of hunger he must have undergone.

But presently the pain of hunger being appeased, he surrendered himself to the pleasure of it, that is, he ceased to be a starved man, and was only a man with a remarkably good appetite, so they began to talk.

Beatrice wondered a little what was the most suitable topic of conversation for a hostess to start, when her guest was a beggar-man off the street; for while it was difficult to find a subject equally inter-esting to both of them, to talk about himself would be as bad as questioning him, and to talk about herself would seem like hinting that she expected him to do the same; but she had her visitor and was bound to entertain him, so she began with a few words about her art. He was quite ready for her.

"Are those your work?" he asked, speaking in a tone that suggested that he hoped she would say no, and glancing at the framed water-colours and crayons hung round the room.

"Oh yes, my School of Art work," she said, with a great deal of scornful apology for them in her tone. "The sort of things they give us to do by way of curing us of any originality or feeling we may have. I don't work like that now."

"No, I don't think you do," he said laughing.

"How do you mean?"

"Well, that was the sort of work you did when you were 'a very good girl,' according to other people's standards; when you always did what you were told, or what other people did; before it occurred to you to think for yourself, act for yourself, and be a good girl, from your own standard. 'Make your soul,' to use a phrase, instead of trying to get it ready-made from a general dealer's. Judging from the little I have seen of you, I should say you were an impressionist now."

"I am," she cried, "heart and soul; that is, I try to draw what I see and feel, and not treat life as mere freehand ornament, more or less projected. May I show you some of my work? Will it bore you?" And starting from her seat she brought forward a big folio, and leant it up against the table.

They looked at the sketches slowly, talking and drinking coffee the while, he praising some frankly, and criticising others just as frankly. He did not know much of painting, of the *technique* that is, but he showed very intelligent ignorance.

"Ah, this is good," he said. "Wait, I think I understand it—Morris, is it not?"

He held a little picture of a fiercely-lighted eastern landscape, with a little indistinct group of armed riders, like the shadow of a cloud blown across it ; she looked over his shoulder at the sketch.

> " I saw the trees in the hot bright weather,
> Clear cut with shadows 'very black,'"

she quoted. "Yes, it is Morris ; do you think I have caught it?"

"Yes. You have got the absolute stillness of noon on to your ten inches of paper ; a stillness these fellows riding emphasise rather than disturb, just as a train, so far off it seems to only creep along the hillside, emphasises the stillness of the Worcestershire hills. Have you ever noticed, by the way, that noon is the only time that ever is still? People talk about the 'hush of evening,' but there isn't any 'hush.' All nature is skurrying home to bed, it is like the suburbwards flight of cabs from Piccadilly Circus on a different scale. There is such a rising of mists, and falling of dew, and shutting up of leaves, and crouching together of grasses, that one can't be quiet ; one can *hear* the night coming on, but the noonday is absolutely still. If I were a ghost, I would choose the noonday, and not the night to revisit the world."

" I've noticed it," she said. " I was staying at a country house in the summer. It was a very high house, and I was at the top of it, and I used to lean out of the window at night, and listen to the grass and leaves folding themselves up for the night. One evening I had such a headache that I could not sleep, so I got out on the parapet, and heard the dew falling below me. It was quite dry, high up, where I was, but below the dew was almost like a rain. There were two people in the garden walking up and down and talking, I could see they were talking, but the rustling of the dew between us shut off their voices, and made it seem like a ghost's pantomime ; it was one of the most unearthly things I ever witnessed. I made a sketch of it, but the perspective is all raving mad. See."

" An impressionist heart and soul," he said. " Yes, indeed you are ; these two doubtless eminently earthly persons look so like ghosts playing at an earthly flirtation that your picture gives one a sensation something like the end of a cold knitting needle drawn down one's back. Are you sure they were earthly people now ? You look like a person who would see ghosts ? "

" Oh, yes," she said laughing, " there was nothing ghostly about them, only about my view of them."

" I knew you were an impressionist before I saw

your work, you know," he went on. "That is why I doubted if those things on the wall were yours; and I should imagine it goes all through you, tastes and feelings and all. You read Pater, don't you?— and Daudet?—especially his shorter sketches. Tourgenieff too, I fancy, even at the risk of depression."

"Tourgenieff breaks my heart," she said; "but I suppose if he didn't it would be because I did not understand him, so I go on reading."

"Take Gyp for comfort, and still go on reading," he said, "your heart will be none the worse in the end, the very end, I mean."

They had closed the portfolio, and pushed away the table by this time. She took a tobacco-pouch from the mantelshelf and began to make cigarettes; he watched her curiously.

"You allow it?" he asked, as the first cigarette being made, she passed it to him.

"Of course, this is Bohemia; haven't you been there before?"

"I have been in many strange places."

"Ah, and I live in Bohemia. I like it, I am not afraid of it, or of any one I meet there."

She turned straight towards him, an unlighted cigarette in her fingers; he leant forward in his chair, looking at her over his tightly folded arms.

"I protest against that aggressive tone," he said, laughing a little. "I don't deserve it, nor you don't need it; you will not be misunderstood in Bohemia, or anywhere else."

She laughed.

"I beg your pardon, you did not deserve it. You have rebuked one of my worst habits. I have an irritating tendency to always stand on my defence. The fact is, I know in my heart, though you may not, that I am rather a dreadful sort of person. I shock most people and distress the rest. I am a perpetual grief to my friends."

The laugh died out as she ended, died down rather, to a smile that was half-scornful, half pathetic. At that moment the door-bell rang, and the smile became almost a sneer.

"Here is another visitor," she said.

She opened the door, and stepped back instantly, letting the new visitor follow her into the room: a man, young, and fairly good-looking, clean-shaven, and with very well-cut features. He was dressed almost fatiguingly well, and an air of almost supercilious prosperity seemed to come into the room with him, and permeate the atmosphere. In his presence the other man's forgotten wretchedness came back on him with a rush; his poverty, his rags, his dirt, overwhelmed him. He was no longer the welcome guest, the sympathetic critic of this sweet, bright girl, but a beggar from the street, fed from charity.

There was a painful silence for a second, then Beatrice spoke.

"Come in, Bert, come nearer the fire; this is a friend of mine, I asked him in to tea. Don't look

so astonished ; you should know by this time that I
have lots of friends besides yourself."

It was small wonder if " Bert " was looking astonished to see this ragged, unkempt, uncanny man so
thoroughly at home and happy in a lady's room ;
but called to himself, answered readily enough, in
what might be called an " elegant " voice :

" Was I looking astonished ?   I don't know why.
You are rather an astonishing person as a rule, but
there is nothing surprising in your having friends to
see you."

This was pretty well for a man taken so completely aback as Rupert Sendal had been ; but the
other guest, still flushed and shamed, looked at
Beatrice with an appeal that had something of
reproach in it.   She responded instantly :

" Oh, he isn't an interloper," she said with a sort
of off-hand graciousness, and indicating Sendal with
a little backward motion of her head.   " He is a
friend of mine, and very nice, really.   Don't disturb
yourself for him, I never do.   He isn't nearly so
prosperous as he looks—fortunately.   In Bohemia
we are all bankrupt alike ; it is only a matter of
degree.   Indeed, I fancy he is the worst off of the
three, for he is in debt ; you and I are spared that
calamity, having no credit.   I don't know how *he*
gets it ; I fancy it is his cuffs.   Those cuffs inspired
me with a simply awful respect for him at first.   The
tradesmen see those immaculate cuffs, and fancy
they mean a conscience, and a banking account to
match.   Poor tradesmen—it's pathetic !"

Sendal dropped into a chair, laughing. If she meant this rattle of nonsense to stand instead of an introduction by name, he might as well accept it. Conversation would be difficult under the circumstances, but less difficult than turning aside one of Beatrice's eccentric moods. She was a dear girl. It was a pity, perhaps, that she did not behave better ; but then, if she did, she would be so much less amusing. As it was, it was so deliciously impossible to know what she would do or say next.

"I don't know," he said lazily ; "I don't know but what in the interests of abstract justice, and from a purely impersonal point of view, I ought not to protest against such a description of myself. It's picturesque, but incomplete."

Beatrice was pleased. Her second guest so far admitted equality with the first that he desired to defend himself before him. She was so pleased with Sendal for following her lead that she spoke his defence herself.

"Oh, it is not his fault, he wouldn't deceive anybody, not even a tradesman to any great extent ; it is quite unconscious, this habit of looking prosperous. He began life as a 'gilded idler,'—you know—'heir of millions,' and that sort of thing, only another heir turned up, one of those superfluous people who always do turn up—the world is full of superfluous people—and now, though he has got into the way of not having any money, he hasn't got into the way of looking as if he had none. I have ; but women are so much more adaptable than men."

"I don't know but what it's good training," said Sendal reflectively ; " to be brought up to the knowledge of how pleasant a thing money is, just as an incentive to make it ; it appeals to one's sense of logic."

"Yes," said the ragged man bitterly. " Send your son to college to learn extravagant habits, and then turn him adrift to support them. It's his own fault if he doesn't make money, you have shown him how necessary it is."

"Your case?" asked Sendal ; he too felt somewhat nearer the man when he had heard his voice.

"Mine ? Oh no, I was thinking of another man, a man I don't know. I was brought up abroad myself. It will always be a matter of regret to me that I was not at Oxford. One makes friends there—one makes friends."

He leaned back loosely in his chair. A look of actual sorrow rose in his eyes, as if he were regretting the friends he had not made. Neither of the others saw the effort it was costing him—had been costing him all the evening—to speak coherently, because the effort had been made so bravely. Beatrice, who had been making more cigarettes, offered one to Sendal.

"Thanks," he said lazily, and lighting it from hers ; then to the other man, " We all smoke here, you see. Are you tolerant of it?"

"Oh, yes. God having made a good thing, I should think it not only selfish but profane to turn to the woman and say, 'He made it for me, but not for you.'"

"But it's not a good thing; it's a 'pleasant vice,' and we men naturally object to women sharing the pleasant vices with us. Haven't we generously given them all the unattractive vices to their share? Why won't they leave us in peace with those from which we can extract a little pleasure? But I see it is no use arguing, she has converted you already."

Beatrice looked up with the same pathetic sneer on her lips.

"He is one of the friends I distress," she said. "I distress him very much."

"Are you distressing him to-night?"

"Oh, I always distress him, but he manages to tolerate me. He would have liked me much better when I painted those," with a gesture towards the School of Art work on the walls.

"My dear child!"

The tone was full of such deep and violent protest that all three laughed, and Beatrice explained.

"Oh, I don't mean for a moment that you like *them*, you are far too cultured not to admire the right thing; but you would have admired the state of soul that painted them, and now I couldn't get back to it, even if I would, I am such a Bohemian."

"You are," said Sendal, "Bohemian from the furthest reach of your soul to the depth of your heart."

The ragged guest spoke absently, as if thinking aloud:

"And that's a great length."

"Yes."   It was an interrogation, and the other answered.

"I mean she has a very wide soul and a very large heart."

"Yes."

It was simple agreement this time; he looked at the girl curiously for a moment as if studying her afresh. It occurred to him that he would very much like to get her out of the room for a moment or two and kiss her. (He didn't put it quite this way for himself: he said, get some explanation of the strange man's presence.) So he asked if he was not to have any coffee.

She laughed an apology for not having offered him any sooner, and suggested that he should go to the kitchen and get the materials, since he knew quite well where they were kept.

He went obediently; they heard him grinding vigorously at the coffee-mill; presently he called to her to come and see if he had ground enough.

She laughed again, understanding perfectly well what he wanted. He might have had the kiss, and welcome, but she was not going to give any explanation of her guest's presence that he did not hear, or that would pain him if he did hear it, so calling back to him to grind a little more to make sure, she went on talking.

Sendal, coming back with the ground coffee, found the other two talking with animation. They had got back to art again, and "Rags," as he christened the other man in his mind, turned and brought him into the conversation as easily and naturally as if he had had ten thousand a year, and had looked as if he had it.

The evening passed very pleasantly for all three after that. Once or twice in the course of it, it occurred to Sendal that the girl's standard of conduct was something infinitely higher and grander than his own rule of behaviour. He began to wonder what he had ever found to tolerate in her.

At last a loud clock, somewhere in the neighbourhood, struck eleven, and each of the three recognised, with a start, that a very pleasant evening was over.

They all three stood up. A troubled look rose in Beatrice's eyes. It was as if she, on the open sea, but knowing her way well, and in a strong boat, had seen some weak swimmer struggling in the water, had brought him into her boat, and kept him safe, but when night came on, being without a *chaperone*, had thrown him back into the sea to drown.

The perplexity on her face deepened into resentment as she looked at Sendal, as if he, being the advocate of conventionality, were responsible for it. He saw her hand slip to her side, and stop short, and knew she was wondering if she might offer her guest money for a night's lodging, but shrank from the coarseness of it.

The ragged guest was speaking in an absolutely conventional tone, there was even an absence of the

gratitude that would have made his dismissal difficult in it.

"We have stayed an unconscionable time; you
have been very good to us.   I have not spent such a
pleasant evening for a long while, I only hope we
have not tired you.   Good-night."

It was impossible for her to offer this man money.
It was as if the rescued man, quietly accepting the
inviolable laws of society, had cheerfully taken his
hat, bowed, and dropped back into the sea to drown.

"You will come with me to-night, won't you?"
Sendal said with real cordiality in his tone; "we have
not half had our talk out, but we can't go on talking
here, because Miss May always turns her visitors out
when it gets late."

"Thank you, I shall be very pleased."

He spoke mechanically, looking the while at
Beatrice, as if accepting the favour solely from her.
Sendal, too, looked to her for the recognition of it.
The two men said good-night, and left the room
together.

It was horribly cold on the landing when the door
was shut behind the two men; "Rags" turned and
watched the gleam of light which they could still
see through the glass above the doorway disappear as
the inner door was shut; even then he made no
movement to go downstairs, but stood leaning
against the rail shivering.

"I shall never see her again."

"Oh, nonsense," said Sendal genially; "Miss May

is not the sort to lose sight of a friend. You will come with me to-night, and to-morrow you will tell us all about yourself, at least all that concerns us— what you have done, and what you can do, you know, and we will see what can be arranged for you."

"You are engaged to her?"

"Yes."

"Do you love her as she deserves?"

"I think I do; because I know now that until to-night I have not."

His words surprised himself; what had come over him that he could speak such a truth to a stranger! The day before he could not have done it, two hours ago he could not have done it, but whatever had caused the change, he knew that it was for the better, and had "come to stay."

They had gone down the first flight of stairs, and now "Rags" had stopped again, with his hand on the rail, and was looking back at the closed door.

"I would die for her."

"You would not be the only one who would do as much," said Sendal.

"Yes. That's nothing—means nothing—tells nothing. I would give my very soul into her hands —I shall never see her again."

"That's a little superlative, isn't it, for one evening's hospitality?"

"It's not for that; it's not for what she did for me, but what she is that I love her."

"Love her?"

"Why not? It can't hurt you. I'm not rivalling you, that's absurd on the face of it. I shall never see her again. How horribly cold it is."

They had got about half way downstairs now, suddenly he stopped short again.

"I don't quite know what I am saying. Have I said anything I should not—anything strange?"

"Oh, lots of strange things, but nothing that one would say you should not. Why, what's the matter? Steady, hold on to me."

For the man's hold on the stair rail had relaxed, he leaned heavily against Sendal, his head drooping on his shoulder, his lips a little apart.

"Hold on to me," said Sendal practically. "Don't be ill here, it is so late, and she lives alone you know. We ought not to have stayed so long—you ought not if you felt ill. Make an effort to get to my rooms, they are close by, we will send for a doctor if you want one when we get there. Don't let us alarm her to-night."

While he was speaking, he had thrown his arms round the man's thin, lank body, and dragged him down the stairs.

The open doorway showed a section of a drenched street, and black wind-tossed rain. Sendal supported his companion against the damp passage wall, while he whistled for a cab.

"It's horribly cold," he said, "how cold you are. Why did you not get nearer to the fire? We'll have some brandy and water when we get to my rooms.

You don't think me a brute, I hope, for not taking you back inside ; but she is all alone you see, and she never will think for herself, so we must think for her. You would not wish to distress her, I know."

"Remember, I would come back from death to serve her."

The wind rushed wet and howling up the passage, mixing with the words, and carrying them away with it. Sendal shivered and shrank up against the wall, grumbling at the cold. The dim lights of the hansom were standing at the entry, the stopping of the wheels had been unhearable in the rain.

"Ah, at last," said Sendal. "Come on. Here, cabby, help me to get him in. You drivelling fool, what are you grinning for ? He's not drunk I tell you, he's ill. Gently, don't haul him like that ; do you think you have hold of a sack of sand ? Be careful with that door, I don't want it on to his fingers, or mine either. Now, as quick as you like to Dennison Street, No. 19."

"Brutes, that they all are," said Sendal, half excusing to himself the anger he could not account for. "Did he hurt you ? Don't trouble to speak though, till we get home, and you have some brandy —hot brandy." He said the words emphatically, as if dwelling with pleasure on the thought of how hot it would be, and shivering, "What a night. This cab is wet through, and as cold as a grave. You shall be out of it in two minutes."

Sendal's rooms were on the ground floor, so it was

easy to carry the man in ; he was rather startled at having to do so, for it showed that the illness must be more serious than he had thought at first, and all the little incidents of the evening had filled him with an interest that was almost affection for this man.

He laid him on the sofa, and proceeded to hunt for the brandy bottle. Everyone seemed asleep in the house, but his fire was still alight ; he stirred it into a blaze, and lit the gas. All the while the man on the sofa never moved.

Sendal came back to him with the brandy.

He was lying straight out on the sofa, his head thrown back on the cushions, his lank black hair falling from his face, his eyes wide open. The brandy Sendal tried to pour through his teeth trickled over his sunken cheek. The man was dead !

Sendal stood staring at him. The brandy was slowly dropping from his lips to the floor. Nothing gives one a more horribly complete realisation of death than the attempt to force the means of life through dead lips. It seems such a desecration to have troubled the dead with the needs of mortality any more—such an insult to their peace.

There was no room for a moment's doubt ; this man was dead, past all aid, and he was alone with him. What was to be done next ?

A doctor must come, of course, if only to certify that his aid was useless ; and the police—in cases like this people always informed the police. It was the work of a moment to wake some inmates of the house, and send the necessary messages, he scarcely had to leave the room to do so; it scarcely interrupted his horrified contemplation of the dead man.

But there was something else to be done. Desolate as this man had seemed, there might still be some one whose right it was to come to him now, to care for him now, and take the ordering of what was to follow. He must find out if this were so.

He must search and find out all Beatrice had abstained from asking, and the man himself had chosen not to reveal. It was horrible. Another desecration; but it had to be done, and Sendal essayed to do it.

The secret, if it was a secret, was easily found. A packet of loosely folded letters lay in his coat pocket. Sendal opened the first.

It began "My dear son," and was signed with the name of his own father.

So this man was his brother, his elder brother, whose unexpected existence had come between him and fortune. His father's son by an earlier and unacknowledged marriage; the man Beatrice had jestingly described as a "surperfluous person," and now he was dead.

His brother, his own brother, whom in the ordinary course of things he should have known and loved. He almost loved him now, as he lay there dead, his thin soiled hands stretched straight out, his face so thin and white, and with such a curious look of resolution on it.

What did it all mean?　His father long ago had quarrelled with him, and had declared the existence of another son who of right was, and should be, his heir.　How indignant he had been at the mere existence of this unacknowledged brother.　Had *he* thought more kindly of the dispossessed brother?　Was it on his own behalf this dead man had spoken so bitterly of the injustice of bringing a man up luxuriously, and leaving him to a life of struggling poverty?　Was it himself he had regretted not having met at Oxford?　Was it really too late for them to love each other?

The room was full of people now, all asking questions.　He collected himself and answered them.

He did not see the need of bringing Beatrice into the affair, supposing it would only be a matter of a few necessary inquiries, so he simply said the man had seemed ill and destitute, so he had brought him home to see what could be done for him, not knowing who he was.

The inspector held out his hand for the letters.

" You should not have touched these," he said.

" Should not I?　I wished to see if he had any friends I might send for."

The inspector was looking at the letters, and did not answer.

" Wilfred Sendal," he read.　" Is that his name?"

" I presume so.　Yes, I am certain of it."

" Do you know the name?"

"Yes. It is the same as my own—the surname at least. He is my half-brother!"

"Your half-brother?"

The inspector glanced at Sendal, then round the room, taking in every sign of comfort and luxury it contained, then at the ragged and starved body stretched out on the couch. Sendal answered the look.

"I did not know him till I saw the letters. I never saw him to my knowledge before to-night. There were family reasons. It is a long story, and this is not the place to tell it. I cannot account for his condition ; he was the heir to property worth half a million."

"Was the heir? Who inherits now?"

"My God, I do," cried Sendal, suddenly realising that it was so.

The doctor looked up suddenly.

"I can give no opinion as to how this man died," he said.

There was an instantaneous change in the manner of the inspector, and of every other person in the room.

"I am afraid this will be serious," said the inspector.

"There will be an inquest?" Sendal turned to the doctor.

"Certainly ; I cannot give a certificate."

"Horrible !"

He looked sadly at his dead brother ; this was yet another desecration.

"I should wire to my father," he said, "but I don't know where he is."

"Your father is Jonas Sendal, of Sendal Court?"

"Yes, but he is never there.   He is travelling."

The doctor looked at him gravely.

" Is it possible you do not know that he is dead?"

"Good God, no.   How do you know it?   Did you know him?"

"I knew of him, most people knew of him, as a great botanist and herbalist.   His death was in the papers to-day."

"Impossible.   What papers?"

"Several.   The death of such a well-known scientist as Jonas Sendal could not pass unnoticed."

"I didn't see it.   They should have sent me word."

"It is natural to suppose you would know."

" This is very serious indeed," said the inspector.

Sendal looked round the room at all the scared condemning faces.

"Speak out plainly," he said.   "You mean—?"

"His death is suspicious," said the inspector, "and you had a great deal to gain by it."

Sendal almost smiled as he looked at his dead brother.   "Poor fellow, he didn't mean this.   Well, sir, it seems idle, and an impertinence to myself to assure you you are mistaken."

" I had better caution you—" began the inspector.

"Oh yes, I know all about that.   What am I to do?"

"We shall have to trouble you to come with us."

"And he?" with a glance towards the sofa.

"My men will see to that matter."

Sendal took a step or two towards his dead brother. He had a strange longing to kiss him, only it seemed ridiculous—theatrical, before so many people. A man must be stirred so very far out of himself before he can kiss another man without awkwardness. A woman would have been different. Sendal had never hesitated about kissing women. Since he had had the right to kiss Beatrice he had wished with a painful regret that he had not kissed so many. He had a foolish fancy that if he were to kiss those dead lips his own would be purified by the touch, so that next time he could kiss Beatrice without self-reproach, but because of the absurdity of the idea he hesitated.

The doctor was looking at him curiously, and spoke with something of regret or apology in his tone.

"I am very sorry for this. I must beg you to believe that I am only doing my duty."

"I am not questioning it."

"And for your own sake it will surely be better that the matter should be thoroughly cleared up."

"I quite agree with you. I am as puzzled as you are. I have certainly more to puzzle me. Any one who helps me to clear up this mystery lays me under an obligation ; he was my brother though I did not know him."

And he fell to wondering what Beatrice would think of the whole affair.

Beatrice scarcely could think of it all as real at first, and yet it did not seem strange, or out of keeping that the incident of the past evening should have an unlikely and unconventional ending. She felt a sort of tender contempt for Rupert's futile effort to keep her name out of the affair. She was sorry that she was to be stared at, questioned and discussed, her freshness and reservedness, her sanctity to him desecrated—her preciousness as a woman deteriorated in his eyes by publicity—sorrier still, that in his eyes this would be so, but such as he was she loved him, so she forgave him, while she grudged that there should be anything to forgive.

She was a little late in reaching the town-hall where the inquest was to be held; two or three people were gathered in the hall discussing the affair; she heard them saying that there would be no *post mortem* till after the inquest had been held, as the inquest might go to show that a *post mortem* was unnecessary. Two or three men came out from a doorway on her left as she entered the room where the inquest was being held; they were talking about " the body."

Still it all seemed more a strange drama than a truth that behind that blank white wall that fronted her as she took her place, the man who had been her guest the evening before lay dead, that her lover was half-suspected of murdering him, and that it was to be left to that fussy, stupid-faced, coarse-handed coroner, and his ignorant jury, to say whether the suspicion should take definite form.

The coroner put on a pair of blue spectacles, and gave a little series of fat murmuring coughs. That seemed the signal for the commencement of the proceedings. The whimsical idea struck her that the coroner was surely not such a remarkably clear-sighted person that he need insist on examining the evidence through those gloomy blue glasses.

They were reading the letters found on the dead man, and could not make very much of them. They were the letters of an angry intolerant father, to an obstinate, and probably wrong-headed son, who apparently would not " give up " something or other. Something which the writer variously alluded to in a *crescendo* of violence from letter to letter as " nonsense," " thorough nonsense," and " infernal nonsense." What the nonsense was the letters did not show, but it was clear that the father declined to give the son any assistance until he made some avowal, or disavowal of belief which the son declared he could not make conscientiously. It seemed at one time during the correspondence the son had turned defiant, for one of the letters taunted him with the fact that he could not raise money on *post obits*, for he could not prove his legitimacy without the writer's assistance, which he should not have. " You have no choice," the letter ended, " but to submit or starve."

Someone interrupted, saying that the letters threw no light on the cause of death, and was snubbed by the coroner for his pains, the letters at any rate proved the identity of the deceased.

Presently it was Beatrice's turn to be examined.

"You are Beatrice May, an artist?"

"Yes."

"Any relation to the deceased?"

"No."

"Nor to his half-brother, Mr. Rupert Sendal?"

"No."

Rupert was watching her, she felt it, though she shrank from looking in his direction, the coroner was still staring at her.

"I am engaged to him," she added proudly.

And Rupert was proud of it too.   Proud in her, and of her, proud that she should stand there before them all, for them to see what manner of woman she was, while she owned herself his; glad of her presence, grateful for her strength and sweetness, and the steadfast words that made him feel he was not alone among this crowd who doubted him. How blind he had been to the best of Beatrice all this while.   It was pleasant to see her so clearly. He hoped he would not be hanged, but it was almost worth while to be hanged for the sake of understanding Beatrice so well.

The coroner was questioning her, but with perfect respect.

"How was it she had asked an utter stranger to her rooms?"

" Because he seemed starving and hungry."

" No. She was not afraid of being robbed by the strange man, she might have been if she had stopped to think, but had thought of nothing but how hungry the man looked. She had not particularly expected to see Mr. Sendal to visit her that evening, but it would have made no difference if she had, she was always willing for him to call when her work was done."

Rupert noticed how sensibly and emphatically she emphasised all the facts that told in his favour. She mentioned how Mr. Sendal had been surprised and half-annoyed to find she had offered hospitality to a stranger, how she had resisted his hints that she should give some explanation of the affair, how she had not introduced Mr. Sendal by name, because that would have entailed enquiry as to the dead man's name, and being sure he was in distress she had thought it might be painful to him to be made to declare himself, and how Mr. Sendal humoured her, and even invited her guest to go to his rooms for the night.

" Then you tell us ? "—the coroner turned one blue disc on Beatrice and the other on Sendal in downright suspicion—" You tell us that Mr. Sendal asked this man to his rooms believing him to be an utter stranger ? "

" Yes, he did it to please me."

It was said so simply, and so modestly, that there was not a man present who did not think the reason sufficient.

When Rupert came forward to give his evidence the feeling of respectful confidence which Beatrice had evoked seemed still in the air, his examination went on smoothly enough at first.

The man was alive when they left Miss May's rooms; he had spoken on the stairway. No, not to reveal his identity, but simply in praise of, and gratitude for, Miss May's kindness. He had not complained outright of feeling ill, but had implied it, exclaiming, " I shall never see her again." Then he had fainted.

"Why had he not returned to Miss May's rooms for assistance?"

"Because it was late, and he did not wish to disturb or frighten Miss May."

"Did he not think that a very trivial reason, in the case of a lady of Miss May's courage and generosity ?"

"Yes, he thought so now. He had thought otherwise at the time, from force of habit, and not realising how seriously ill the man was."

"You thought, in fact, of trivial conventionalities, which Miss May herself was too sensible and good to consider, while your own brother was dying ?"

"I am ashamed to say that I did, but I had no more idea that he was dying than I had that he was my brother."

"You say he fell against you—helpless, into your arms on the way downstairs ?"

"Yes."

"Did not that make you think him seriously ill?"

"Yes, but not dangerously. I thought he was simply overcome with fatigue, and the humiliation of his position and—" Rupert was losing his self-control somewhat as the scene came back to him. "He felt Miss May's conduct deeply; he was quite unmanned by it; he spoke strangely."

Beatrice, staring at the coroner, saw doubt of Rupert's word in every line of his commonplace face, in the heavy mouth, the obstinate chin, in all the self-satisfied wrinkles round his eyes; only the blue spectacles were unmoved. She seemed to see it all happen, see her own landing—the fading light—and in the dark hear the two men talking about her.

The coroner was speaking.

"Miss May told us that your invitation was given through her influence. Does that mean at her request?"

"No, but I knew that it would please her."

"You only did it with that view?"

"No, before the end of the evening I was deeply interested in this man—my half-brother. But I suppose that but for her influence it would not have occurred to me. That is as near as I can get. I can't answer questions in metaphysics."

"We don't want metaphysics," the coroner answered severely. "We only want facts, but we must get at them in our own way. You say he fell helpless in your arms. Go on from that. What happened next?"

"He was very heavy. I got him downstairs, and we leaned against the wall, while I called a cab. He was very heavy, and very cold. He spoke again then."

He looked at Beatrice, listening, bent forward in her seat. Her thoughts seemed more with the scene he described than with his present words, her eyes, fixed steadfastly on the coroner and her lover, changed with every question and answer.

The coroner was speaking.

"And he was dead when you reached your rooms?"

"I found then that he was dead."

"You assume that he died in the cab?"

"I don't know."

"When do you think he died?"

"If you ask me what I think—?"

He stopped short.   It was clear to everyone in the court that he was losing his self-control.   He seemed scarcely able to command his voice or his memory.   "If you ask me what I think—?"

"We wish to have your impression."

"I don't know when he died."

"Did you feel no change when you were supporting him in the cab?"

"No change since he fell in my arms on the stairs.   He turned very cold then, so did I.   I turned cold at the touch of him."

"But you say he spoke again after he fell in your arms?"

"Yes, I said so."

His excitement, his nervousness, the hesitation with which he spoke, were all telling against him, and the antagonism of his hearers took form in a general glance of sympathy towards Beatrice. He turned towards her to see if she understood it—if she knew that these people were all sorry for her because they believed her lover was a murderer. It seemed as if she did. It seemed as if in a moment it had all grown real to her, as if now she knew at last that this was no show, no pageant, but a real thing, as real as it was horrible, that her lover was in danger, might be lost to her, and he saw a moment's agonised outcry rise in her face. "*I can't do without him.*" The words did not pass her lips, he did not hear them, but he knew of them as well as if they had been said loud for the whole world to hear. He began to feel very much more sorry for Beatrice than for himself. She had flung herself forward in her seat, listening with terrible intentness.

The coroner was speaking.

"You have not told us what he said when he spoke again."

"*I would come back from death to serve her.*"

He looked at Beatrice as he spoke the words, half ashamed of troubling her with the repetition of them, they seemed such a mockery now. There was something cynically humorous in quoting such words from the dead man, who had felt and spoken such deep gratitude to her, and who, now lying still and white and silent behind that wall, had brought all this upon those who had befriended him.   She had not moved.   Still bending forward in her seat, still with the same curiously intent look on her face, she seemed repeating the words softly to herself. She scarcely noticed him.   He felt as if he had lost her for a moment.

There were other witnesses.   The doctor to tell how he was unable to account for the cause of death.   It might be heart disease accelerated by hunger and exposure, or even hunger and exposure alone, but he could not be sure till after the inquest *post mortem.*   He seemed to think it absurd that the inquest should have been held at all till after the *post mortem,* and hinted that the police had acted very stupidly.

Then there was the inspector to tell how Sendal had denied all knowledge of his father's death, though he had been reminded that it had been in the papers.   Of course a journalist might be expected to know everything that appeared in every paper, so much was clear to every thick-headed juror, who, had he been asked how many papers altogether there were in existence to read, would have been utterly unable to give an answer.

Then the cabman had to testify to his unprovoked anger and excited manner, and the coroner stretched forward, thrusting his hideous blue spectacles between him and Beatrice, questioning the man, encouraging him, seeming as if he thought it his special mission to fix guilt on her lover.

Did not Beatrice care? Had she forgotten him? Were all her thoughts behind that wall where, stretched out still and motionless, lay the man who had said he would come back from the grave to serve her?

Rupert, looking at her still intent face, felt as if he had lost her altogether. The business of the inquest went on. There were other witnesses to be examined. Everything seemed telling against him. He was suddenly startled to realise how little hope he had. Only he wished it was all over.

Well, it soon would be all over, and clearly it would end badly for him. The coroner was giving a few more little prefatory coughs; the police inspector was scribbling some order on a torn leaf of a note book.

Suddenly Beatrice rose from her seat with a cry, and then stood silent, one hand outstretched towards the wall, every one waited amazed. What was she about to say?

She spoke quietly, steadily, but with long pauses between her words.

"He has risen. His eyes are open. He is speaking. Go to him."

Then she dropped back in her seat. Some of the officials, thinking her ill, hurried forward to help her from the place. Some, who were near the door, crept out from that room to the next, and rushed back exclaiming that it was true, the man was alive.

The doctor and the jury hurried into the next room. Rupert and as many of the spectators as could push past the officials followed.

Wilfred Sendal had raised himself on one elbow, and brushing back the lank hair from his forehead, was staring puzzled round the room.

"What is all the fuss about?" he said.

The doctor came forward with a restorative; he pushed it away.

"What is the matter, what do you want to know?"

The doctor tried to stop the questioning coroner; the man protested.

"I'll not be moved, I'll not be moved or doctored. Let me speak. I shan't be here long, I must speak. You tell me," turning to Rupert. "What does it all mean?"

He was not looking at him, his eyes were utterly vacant, the doctor, thinking it better to humour him, signed to Rupert to come near and speak.

"I am accused of murdering you, you were found dead in my rooms."

"Why should you murder me? I was dying as it was."

"I am your younger brother, Rupert Sendal, and I had much to gain by your death."

"Yes, my brother, but you did not kill me. Cold

and hunger killed me."   His voice, clear but faint, gave signs of failing; he turned, still with the same vacant eyes, to the crowd.

" I love them, these two, as they love each other; no harm must come to them.   I was dying of starvation when she found me.   The food and drink I had in her house I saw her prepare, and she shared it.   Nothing passed my lips after I left her door.   Is everyone satisfied ? "

" You have freed your brother from suspicion," said the doctor, " now think of yourself; drink this."

" No, leave me alone, I have done my work."

His head dropped back on the cushion some one had brought, his vacant eyes still wandered round the room, Rupert leaned forward to take his hand, he looked up.

" Tell her I did it," he murmured.

.   .   .   .

Half-an-hour later, Sendal, free from all suspicion, was waiting with Beatrice at a side door, for the cab he had sent for to take her home.   She had lost her courage now, and was clinging to him, crying a little.

" It's all over, dear," he said.   " Be your brave self again.   God knows how I wish the poor fellow had lived, we should have loved him."

" We can still."

" Yes.   I am puzzled.   It has all been very sad, and very strange.   I never knew him, but I grudge to give him up to death.   We owe him a great deal, Beatrice.   I have learnt much from all this, and so have you, I think."

"Yes," and her hold on him strengthened.

The doctor came down the passage.   He came straight up to Sendal and spoke frankly.

"You are going?   Wait one moment.   This is a strange affair, Mr. Sendal.   Do you make any complaint against me?"

"No."

"I suspected you, helped to point suspicion against you.   Have you nothing to say against me for giving your living brother up for dead?"

"No."   Sendal's voice was puzzled and half afraid, as it had been when he answered the coroner.

"Mr. Sendal, if a young man, a novice—oh! I'll be frank, if anyone but myself had made such a blunder I should have thought and spoken very severely."

He hesitated ; Sendal was looking at him curiously but not hostilely.   He went on :

"But if his life had been the dearest on earth to me, I must have said the same, if my own life had depended on it, I must have said the same—the man was dead."

Sendal spoke with the air of a man who half fears the import of his own words, yet cannot withhold them.

"Was it a blunder?   Did you notice what he said ? Cold and hunger *killed me.'*   There is something very strange about it all."

He hesitated, looking at Beatrice, the doctor's eyes followed his. The dead man's strange impossible promise rose in the minds of each of the three, but none of them spoke it aloud.

The doctor looked at them, troubled and puzzled. "I am a scientific man," he said, "and my science told me he was dead. As you say, it is, all very strange."

"Yes ; can you explain it ?"

"No. I can give you scientific names for the cause of his death, for his—revival—but I can't explain it, I can't explain it."

JOHN O'NEAL'S HONOUR.

John O'Neal's Honour.

ALL men are brothers. This remark has been made before, and will have to be made many times again before people begin to believe it. In a very large family it is natural that the members should exercise some favouritism in their affection, it is scarcely possible to love all alike, and in this big human family we occasionally find some of our relatives distinctly unlovable, and some so much better off than ourselves that they have no claim whatsoever on our sympathies. For undoubtedly the greatest claim anyone can urge on our love is the need of it. That counts, or should count, for even more than the desire of it. It is easier to feel the reality of our brotherhood with such as are ill-off, hopeless, or sad, and appeal to what is best in us, than with such as are arrogantly and blatantly prosperous, and neither care in the least for our brotherhood, nor scruple to show us how little they care. It is easier to see Christ in the man we pity than in the man we envy. When Dives rolls past in his carriage, spattering our carefully-kept clothing with mud, openly scorning us and our brotherhood alike, we are apt to forget that he, too, has a soul, and that somewhere in that big mass of insolent prosperity there is a human heart, however hardened by selfishness, or smothered in luxury. But to Lazarus we can say with Lowell—

> "I behold in thee
> An image of Him who died on the tree ;
> Thou also hast had thy crown of thorns,
> Thou also hast had this world's buffets and scorns,
> And to thy life were not denied
> The wounds upon the hands and side."

And therefore, if I have wronged my brother Dives, the fault sits lightly on me ; he does not care, so I need not distress myself; but to wrong my brother Lazarus is a different matter.

Now, I have been wronging one of my brothers lately, and as, now the cold weather has set in, I fear I shall never see him any more, for the sake of the family honour I want to apologise to all his brothers and mine.

I was very fond of John O'Neal. He used to come round with the coal cart in the mornings, and bring me my coals up to the top flat where I live ; up four flights of rather steep stairs that means. I am by no means a prosperous or aristocratic person. I live in a little flat near Chelsea Station, and work there very hard, illustrating cheap periodicals ; but my studio is very pretty. I made most of my furniture, it is true, out of empty sugar boxes and egg cases, disguised in stamped American leather and art muslin, but the result is a distinct success. The effect when one first comes in at the door is very good indeed, and gives one a sensation of light and colour that is exhilarating in this gloomy weather.

The room looks like a studio, and does not betray the fact that it is occasionally used as a kitchen, for I keep my litter out of sight, and my dearly-loved Venus of Milo—how I wish I had not to call her by that idle name, so out of harmony with the gentle grandeur of the dear goddess of all woman-hood and motherhood—she will not tell that behind the dull rich drapery against which she stands is the coal cellar, in the shape of an old oak tea chest, in which I keep my bi-weekly allowance of coals—half a hundredweight.

From the very first morning when John O'Neal brought up my coals I felt the relationship between us. Something even in the pathetic baritone in which he called " Co-oals, Co-o-ALS ! " attracted me, as I ran to the window, and made the sign of the cross with my two first fingers (the signal, in these vulgar regions, that you only want half a sack ; if you want a whole one, hold up one finger). When he got as far as my door he stood a moment, looking into the room astonished, and glancing dubiously at his feet, as if regretting that he had not wiped his muddy boots on someone else's door-mat down below. Then he came in slowly over the waxed floor, and stopped in the middle of it, looking round with a puzzled admiring air, as if to ask, " Where in all this strange place, so utterly un-like anywhere else that I visit in my morning rounds, do you keep anything so unlovely and commonplace as coals ? "

I showed him the nook behind the Venus, and asked him to try not to make a dust. An un-necessary precaution ; he poured out the coals as carefully as I pour out tea into my best eggshell china, and rolled up the sack promptly, so that no dust should drop off it. I gave him sixpence-half-penny (coals were cheap then), and he began to walk very slowly out of the room. I had time to see what he was like, to notice a brilliant com-plexion, and big hollow eyes, hands that, dirty and knotted as they were, seemed as if nature had made them for playing sweet music, or writing sad poems, rather than carrying dirty sacks about. John O'Neal was beautiful, with that intense beauty that is only found among peasants, people who work with their bodies—beauty both of form and of colour. An idle man could never have had those fine, clear-cut features, and sharp outlines. A brainworker could not have had those finely-developed limbs and straight shoulders, not that rich glowing colour. All the same John O'Neal did not look a healthy man, and I felt very sorry for him, even while the practical idea ran through my mind that, were I ever in want of one, he would make an incomparable model.

All this while he was on the way to the door. He stopped there for a last glance.

"Good morning," I said civilly.

He began to say good morning, but stopped to cough. By the time he had finished coughing, he had forgotten that he was going to say anything, and went downstairs, coughing all the way, I supposed from bashfulness, for my room and my greeting together seemed to have bewildered him.

After that I began to feel quite friendly with John O'Neal. He liked my room and I liked him: it was a fair exchange. I used to listen for his soft pathetic baritone, and decline all offers of coal from anyone else. I soon found out that the cough and the complexion did not mean bashfulness, but consumption, and that John O'Neal knew it. Not that we ever spoke to each other, beyond the ordinary exchange of business courtesies—"Good morning," "Coals is up," "Have you change?" and so on— but from his sad eyes, and gentle hopelessness, I was sure that he knew, and I was very sorry for him.

This was in the early autumn. In October I lost sight of my friend. Perhaps his master had changed his district; at any rate he did not come down my street for some time; but in November, during that sudden burst of bitter weather, in answer to my sign at the window, John O'Neal came to my door

It had been sleeting, and the half-frozen sleet was crusted round the edge of the sack, and round the collar of his ragged coat and the rim of his hat. He had grown thinner, much thinner, but his cheeks were as brilliant and his eyes as patient as ever. His cough was much worse.

I said that it was a cold morning, and he agreed with me, breathlessly, because it had taken all his breath to carry that sack up four flights of stairs (I wonder how he felt after carrying the hundred-weights). I was just breakfasting, so I offered him a cup of coffee.

He took it eagerly, holding my pretty cup almost reverently in his bony black hands, with the thin wrists, and knuckles that looked like knots in old rope. I said that he had a very bad cough, and he answered "Yes, miss;" but there was no time for sympathetic conversation—the cart was waiting for him. Coals had gone up to one and twopence. I looked in my purse for sixpence and a penny, but found only a penny and a shilling.

"Have you change?" I asked.

He had not, but his mate down at the cart had. He would bring it.

But it seemed a pity to make this tired, consumptive man toil all the way up the stairs again. So I gave him the shilling and the penny, and told him that if he put fivepence in coppers just inside the common door downstairs, close against the wall, I should find it the first time I went out.

He looked very much obliged to me for saving him trouble, even more so than he had been for the coffee; but he only said "Yes, miss," and went downstairs coughing.

I was sorrier for him than ever. It can't be a pleasant calling to walk round through shabby little streets with a coal cart, even in fair weather. It must be hard work, even for a healthy man, to carry hundredweights and half-hundredweights of coal up limitless stairs at one and twopence a hundred; and now the weather was cruel, and John O'Neal was ill, and to have to do such work for such pay; I don't know how much exactly, but it is plain it cannot be much when one considers what has to come out of that sevenpence, or one and twopence, as the case may be. First, the royalty to the landlord on whose property the mine is; then the interest on the cost of the plant for working a mine; the wages of the workmen, overseers, and clerks employed in the mine; the charge of the railway company for carriage to London; the interest on the cost of the horse, coal waggon, and sack (this latter costs half-a-crown, John O'Neal told me, or at any rate that is what the men are fined if they lose one); the keep of the horse, and the wages of the driver. From all this it is plain that John O'Neal's share of that sevenpence for carrying the coals upstairs could not be much.

I thought this over, and all the morning, while I was working, I could not get John O'Neal's thin face, and hollow eyes, his terrible cough, and voice that was growing so harsh and weak, out of my mind. But when, later in the day, I went downstairs, and looked for that fivepence in coppers, there was no trace of it.

I asked the people who lived downstairs if they had seen it, but they had not; indeed, when I explained the circumstances of the case they seemed to think it absurd that I should suppose anyone would ever see that fivepence, and hinted politely that I must be little better than an idiot to trust a coalman.

I was loath to doubt John O'Neal. I asked if there had been any message boys to the door that morning. I should not have been much surprised if I had had to suspect a message boy, because a message boy has not had time to develop a conscience; besides, none of the message boys were my personal friends. It would not have hurt me (except on the general grounds of love of honesty, and loss of cash) if one of them had taken it; but my brother was different—"I hadn't thought it of him." That is what makes so many wrongs bitter—"we didn't think it" of the wronger. But the message boys were innocent, it seemed. The lady downstairs assured me that every time anyone had come to the door that morning she had answered it herself, and therefore no one could have taken the coppers if they had been put there as I had directed. The man could not have left the money.

Well, coalmen might be all alike. That particular man was not bound to be immaculately virtuous because he had a cough; but whomsoever he had cheated, he should not have cheated me, because I had trusted him.

I hoped for two or three days that he had merely forgotten, but at last I lost faith in him. I tried to forgive him, I tried to convince myself that I had no right to expect anything better of a man who had never professed any high standard of honour. I told myself that, had I been bred in the slums, and passed my days carrying coals up four flights of stairs at sevenpence a half-hundred, I should very likely have done the same. Who had ever taught honour and chivalry to John O'Neal? He had never read Kingsley's essay on "Heroism," nor Lowell's Poems, nor McCarthy's novels, nor Matthew Arnold, nor "The Light of Asia," nor any of the grand and beautiful teaching that has not made me, myself, anything so very wonderful in the way of uprightness after all. What right had I to judge John O'Neal?

But it was no use reasoning with myself. I couldn't whiten his fault; it would look black, for all my reasoning—black as his own coals. It was no use saying I would not judge him; I did judge and condemn him. I was glad he did not come round with the cart any more. I did not want to see him again. My brother had disappointed me, and it is no exaggeration to say that I was deeply grieved.

I told myself that in my foolish, romantic way I had been idealising an ordinary commonplace and unprincipled man, just because he had a bad cough, and a beautiful complexion, and so resolved to think no more of him.

But a few days ago I saw John O'Neal again. It was when the fine weather came back for a day or two, and the sleet and frost had disappeared, and a warm wind dried up the streets. I was going out somewhat early in the morning, and on opening the common door downstairs I found him on the steps. He was thinner and more hollow-eyed than ever, and he looked at me with a sad friendly smile,—

"Coals, miss?"

His voice was almost a whisper now—that was why, probably, I had not heard it in the streets—and he leaned languidly against the doorway while he spoke.

I wanted to speak about that fivepence. I wanted to say, "Look here, my friend, is it right, is it prudent, to say the least, for a man on the brink of the grave as you are, to sell his soul for a miserable fivepence?" But I could not; the accusation would have pained him so much if it were false, and me so much if it had been true. I did not want any coals, but I could not let him go without a word, so I asked him where he had been the last week or two.

"Laid up," he croaked curtly. And he turned to go.

But I was not going to shirk my duty. I must not encourage dishonesty; I have a conscience, so I compromised with it.

"One moment," I said, speaking cheerfully and carelessly. "By the way, did you not forget that fivepence?"

"Fivepence, miss?" He reflected, and remembered. "It weren't fivepence; it was sixpence. You giv' me a shillin' and a penny, and the coals was sevenpence, then."

"Where did you put it?"

He pulled the door half shut, and pointed behind it.

"Down there."

There was nothing visible, so I stooped, and turned up the edge of the matting, and there among the dust, lay a very dirty sixpence; and I believe not even the sight of the cheque I received in payment for my first picture gave me more pleasure than did the sight of that shabby little coin.

"That's all right," I said, cheerfully. "I thought you had forgotten it."

This was not true, but I don't think that the recording angel entered it against me. I wanted to hide my pleasure, as I hid my disappointment, that John O'Neal might not see how I had doubted his honour.

Does he know now? I wonder, for we parted then with a friendly word or two, and he does not come round with the coals any more. Does he know, now, up where he is?   Ah! well, if he does, he will forgive me ; dead people should forgive us easily, they have so much the best of it.

I don't think I am sorry that John O'Neal is dead when I think of his cough and the cold weather.   He had a hard time of it here, but

"The day is aye fair, in the land of the leal."

BELIEVE IT NOW.

BELIEVE IT NOW.

CHAPTER I.

GERTRUDE SOUTHEY.

"SHALL I ever believe you love me?"

He looked up lazily from among the long grass and fern under the trees in the old orchard, half surprised, half amused.

"What's the difficulty?" he said, "you are pretty —almost as pretty as people have made you think yourself—you are very charming, and fairly intelligent, why should you find any difficulty in believing that I, who rather pique myself on my good taste, if on no higher quality, should love you?"

"It is not that," she answered impatiently; "oh, no, I have a sufficiently high opinion of myself, I assure you. I don't doubt that I might be loved, but I doubt whether you love me."

"Then don't doubt any more, take my word for it, I ought to know."

"I did take your word for it, when I gave you mine."

"Are you going to say you regret it?"

"No, no, not that, but there is something I do regret."

"In me? Well yes, I am afraid there is a good deal to regret in me, or to forgive. Can't you do it?"

"What can you do in return?"

"Why love you. Is that not enough?"

It might have been enough if she had believed it, but she was not sure. She leaned back against a tree trunk, looking at her lover with a shadow in her eyes, puzzled, and not understanding her own discontent.

"Well," he said presently, "what are you going to say next? I think we have been very happy since we have been engaged, or been going to be engaged, which is it? If you will think anything so unnatural as that I do not love you, might you not just as well wait until I give you some confirmation of the idea before you begin to fret over it? For my part I have not any doubts whatever. I should be supremely contented if you were."

"But I am not," she said sadly, "I wish I were, but I am not."

"Are you discontented with me? What have I done?"

"Nothing," she said sharply, "you will never do anything."

"Oh! that's it, is it?" he said with a little laugh. "Well, no, I suppose I never shall. I don't know of anything that I could do. I can't promise like Montrose to 'make you famous by my pen, and glorious by my sword.' I have not got any pen, nor any sword either, and if I had I should not know what to do with them. It is a pity, but I cannot be other than I am—I am afraid I should say more than I am; I think nature must have been short of material when she made me, for she did not make very much of me. I wish that I were more for your sake, but all there is of me loves you very dearly. Does not that please you?"

"Please me? Yes. But what is it to be pleased, if one is not satisfied?"

"I wish I could satisfy you—as fully as you satisfy me; I fancy that I shall some day, but meanwhile, I wish I were a hero, or a poet, or an artist, or anything great for your sake, but I am not, and I cannot be, even you cannot make a hero of me; but, my dear, if you cannot make me great, is it not enough that God has made me true?"

He rested his hand on hers among the long grasses, and looked up into her face. The girl did not speak, but she let her hand lie quietly in his, and her eyes filled with tears.

"You are very sweet and good," she said at last. "Do you mind my using words to praise you that are generally kept for us women? You *are* sweet and good, and very patient with me, and you are very true too. I could not doubt your truth, whatever else I doubted. You could not deceive me, but you might fail me."

He laughed.

" Wait and see if I do."

"Oh, I don't mean that if I agree to a real engagement you may change your mind and jilt me—you would not do anything so horribly ill-bred. I see the very word makes you wince. Besides I doubt if you would have the vigour to do such a thing; the cruelty of it would shock you so. And I know that you would be a good husband, you would never be unkind or harsh." Here she stopped and laughed. The idea of harshness seemed so incongruous in connection with her lover's slight figure, beautiful, delicate face, and insipid, little, fair moustache. "Oh, I know you will be very good to me," she went on, " far too good ; but—there is something that I miss. Perhaps the fault is in myself, not in you. I wish you would complain of me a little, Gilbert."

" I can't, my dear, unless I were to grumble that you do not love me enough."

" I should borrow your own words, ' All there is of you I love very dearly.' There is nothing in you that I do not like ; but—" she stopped short, laying her hands appealingly on her lover's arm, "complain of me, too, Bertie, pray complain of me ; there is so much that is unlovable in me, won't you tell me of it ?"

"There is nothing I do not love, not even your very faults nor your hardness—for you have faults, and you are hard sometimes. Truly, women are much crueller than we are, always. No man would taunt the woman he loved with want of beauty as you taunt me with want of strength."

"Don't forgive me then, don't be patient with me, don't be kind."

"I had rather ; but I think you should be more kind to me."

"Is it not better to be true than kind ? Would you not rather know just exactly how I feel—that is if I could know myself—so that you might decide if it is worth while going on ?"

"Of course it is worth while 'going on' as you lucidly express it. You have a gloomy fit to-day ; you are not yourself. I think there is a thunder-storm coming on (I hope by the way it won't come soon enough to spoil Lady Morley's ball to-night.) You very resolute people always suffer more than we who are weaker, when you have a moment's doubt, just as very healthy people make a fuss over a trifling pain which a chronic invalid wouldn't deign to notice. The heat is melting you into irresolution ; shake it off—be yourself again. Are we not always happy together ? We don't bore each other ; we never quarrel ; and did you not say three weeks ago that you loved me ?" O

"I said that I thought so. I do think so."

"And do I not love you?"

"Do you? That is just what I want to know. You see I take things so much more in earnest than you do. You don't seem ever to look at anything seriously."

"I am not a very serious person, but I love you, Gertrude, really I do."

"I suppose I shall believe it some day."

"Believe it now. The thing rests with yourself; you are not content because you do not believe in my love? Well, believe in it, for it is honestly worth your belief. Trust me as I trust you, and then you will be as thoroughly satisfied as I am myself."

"You are satisfied?"

"Yes. I shall be more satisfied though when you will own to the engagement publicly."

"Does that mean that you think I shall be more likely to keep my promise if people know of it?"

She spoke quickly but not angrily, more as if eager to know the exact feeling that prompted the words than resenting them.

"No, not that; not that by any means. Only, as you have once or twice reminded me, the promise made to me was not very definite. You said you *thought* that you loved me. You *thought* that you would marry me. When you publish the engagement I shall know you are sure. When will you publish it, Trudie?"

His gentleness and patience touched her; she felt ashamed of her vague dissatisfaction, besides she was really very fond of her lover, so after a moment's hesitation she answered steadily,

"To-night."

His face lit up with pleasure, but with amusement too.

"To-night? At Lady Morley's? How shall you do it? Stand up in the middle of the room and announce: 'I hereby give notice that I have accepted an offer of marriage from Gilbert Ashley; and anyone who thinks slightingly of him in the future will have to answer for it to ME.' You are quite capable of such a thing in your valiant moods. I think I should rather like it, but it would be trying to one's nerves. I should feel honoured but embarrassed."

She laughed.

"I am not nearly so valiant as you think, Gilbert, you will find that out soon. You will make that, and many another disappointing discovery some day. No, I shall tell mother before I go out to-night, she will not be surprised, she knew we were thinking of it. She is not well enough to come with me to Lady Morley's, but that does not matter, as we know Lady Morley so well, and her house is only a step or two from ours. I will tell her in the course of the evening, and then you can bring me home. That will be enough, will it not? You can tell as many of your own friends as you like to-morrow."

"There won't be anything left to tell, by the time dear old Lady Morley has had the news half an hour," he said cheerfully. "Thank you, Gertrude. What a practical girl you are, and how pretty you look when you are considering ; you don't wrinkle your eyebrows out of their proper place, as most people do."

"I must go in now," she said, "it is time for the boys to have their tea."

"Can't they have it without you ? "

"Well, yes, but they don't like it if I am not there."

"I see," he said admiringly, but a little resentfully too. "Nothing in the house, from a lawsuit to bread and butter, can get on without you. What your people will do when you are married Heaven only knows—unless indeed, you decide merely to group me in along with the rest, as one of the many weaklings dependent on your superior strength."

A pathetic look rose in her eyes, and her lips trembled. She seemed for a moment as if about to protest, almost tearfully against his judgment of her, but changing her mind held out her hand, only saying "Good-bye." They had risen now, and he was brushing the grass from his coat with his gloves.

"Good-bye. Let me see, are we really engaged now ? or will that only be to-morrow ? "

"To-morrow," she said lightly ; "it cannot be a really formal engagement until all the dear old gossips in the place have talked it over."

"But you will kiss me now, Trudie?"

Yes she would, and she moved a step or two nearer, and he laid his hands on her shoulders.

"You are sure of my love now," he said, with actual triumph in his voice, "now you will let me kiss you."

But as his lips touched hers, and he looked lovingly into her eyes, he saw there was still something of which she was not sure. The sight did not distress him, he was to have the opportunity of proving his love, and he was very sure of it himself. He went away laughing at the absurdity of such a girl doubting in such a matter, and thinking how differently she would kiss him some day.

CHAPTER II.

OWEN O'RUAC.

LADY MORLEY was distinctly the great lady of the place, and her ball, given on the anniversary of her wedding day, which unfortunately fell in the middle of August, was the great event of the little country neighbourhood in which she lived.

This year, her favourite nephew, Owen O'Ruac, who always came to stay with her for the occasion, and always grumbled at it, declared emphatically that the heat being phenomenal, even for August in a south-eastern county, he would strike work, shirk the ball, and go and sit in the mushroom house until it was all over unless his aunt would agree to have the thing out of doors.

He pointed out that the lawn was as dry as tinder with the heat, and as slippery as any waxed floor. The shrubberies and pathways would look well lighted up with lamps, the nights were quite as hot as the day just then, so no one could possibly catch cold; moreover a ball in the garden would not give half as much trouble to the servants, either before or afterwards, as a ball in the house.

Lady Morley had agreed, and when the evening came only wondered that she had never thought of giving an out-door ball before.

Gertrude Southey was one of the most popular girls in the neighbourhood ; she had so many friends to speak to, and so much to say to them that Ashley had very little of her company during the earlier part of the evening, but he was quite contented to amuse himself with one or two of her friends till she had leisure to attend to him. Far too happy to feel bored or impatient, he wandered about from one group to another watching Gertrude with loving admiring eyes all the time.

Presently he saw her notice that Owen O'Ruac was standing near ; and he saw her start and turn with such a distinct and palpable expression of pleasure on her face as made Owen O'Ruac leave the group of men with whom he had been talking, and hurry across to her, and she, though she had not yet quite carried out her well-behaved intention of speaking to everyone she knew, especially to all the girls, before she began to enjoy herself, left the last of her friends neglected, and began to walk up and down the half-lighted paths with him.

Ashley was not of a jealous disposition, but he did feel a moment's regret that he was not more like O'Ruac. As big, and as vigorous, with the same resolute chin, and decided jaw-bone—the same big powerful hand, that looked for all the world as if nature had intended it to be doubled up and used for a coal-hammer, but which, nevertheless, could make tiny fishing flies with a skill and dexterity a professional might have envied, and nurse a sick child as tenderly as a woman.

But, if Ashley envied the other's glorious physique it was only for a moment. Had not Gertrude chosen him as he was?

Lady Morley signed to him to come and be introduced to some new arrivals, and he lost sight of Gertrude and O'Ruac.

They had been talking together for nearly half an hour, and now they were standing at the end of a long walk, leaning against a wooden paling.

"Yes," Gertrude was saying with a laugh, "I remember that I did just the same the last time I saw you. It is very ill-bred of me to show my feelings so openly. Does it amuse you that I let you see so plainly that I like to talk to you?"

"No," he said, "but it surprises me a little, and pleases me a great deal."

The very tone of the man's voice had an emphatic ring in it, giving one the idea that he always knew exactly what he thought, and thought it very thoroughly. As Gertrude did not speak, he asked:

"Why is it?"

His manner was not rough, or even abrupt; on the contrary it was courteous and pleasant, but there was so much force in it that almost involuntarily Gertrude answered candidly, perhaps too candidly,

"I think it is because you are the strongest character I ever met in my life."

He laughed a healthy emphatic laugh, throwing up his chin, and showing two perfect rows of savagely white teeth as he did so.

"That should make you dislike me, if there is anything in contrast of character, according to the reputation you have in the neighbourhood."

"Ah, that's just it," she said impulsively; "my reputation is all wrong. Can't you conceive of a person being driven by circumstances into a character utterly different from anything nature intended? By some strange chance all the people I know and love are weaker than I am myself, so I have to *be* strong if I can, and *seem* so if I cannot. The effort hurts me sometimes. My mother depends on me, I had very much rather depend on my mother; and it is the same with most of my friends. They all think me strong and self-reliant, and I am neither, or if I have become so by habit I regret it. You see, having no father, my mother being an invalid, and I the eldest of so many, I have always *had* to take the lead, so I have taken it. Everyone thought that I was so sensible and practical and steadfast in the matter of that lawsuit, but if they had known the days and nights of anxiety, the agonies of doubt I underwent when I had persuaded mother to take my advice, they would have thought very differently. You see, if I had shewn any weakness at that time mother would have been afraid to follow my counsel, and then we should have been almost beggars, instead of being tolerably well off, as we are now."

"If you are not strong you must be very brave," he said.

"I don't know about that either. Desperation is not courage. I once heard of a girl who, knowing nothing of the sea, put out in a small boat on a very rough day because she saw other people on the bay, and so thought she would be safe enough. The other people were men who knew the coast and had been used to boats almost before they could walk, and this girl soon found out that she could not manage her boat at all, and got frightened. She wanted to get back to the pier, but what with the wind and the waves and the tide she actually did not dare to turn round lest she should be swamped. So she kept the boat's head straight with the wind, and rowed boldly *across* the bay, left her boat in the care of a fisher, and came home by train. That girl gained a reputation for simply reckless courage by what was really the merest exercise of prudence. I did something of the same sort. I saw we should inevitably be ruined if someone did not find a mind and make it up, so, as there was no one else to do it, I did it myself; but I did not like doing it."

"That's where the courage comes in. You'll have to admit one virtue or the other, Miss Southey; the less you are strong, the more you are brave to act strongly."

" No," she said, "I am a fraud, I feel it, but it is not quite my fault; I have always had to play up to the reputation I made then. I hope I shall not be found out; at least, not by anyone weaker than myself. It would be a calamity indeed if I failed anyone who relied upon me. Oh! I shall keep my reputation as long as I can; but, as I have said, it is trying. Have you ever seen those sandbags that the old women in cottages lay along the window-sashes to keep out the draught?"

"Yes: heaps of them. Why?"

"Oh! because it is a useful enough piece of furniture, and happy enough, doubtless, so long as it lies along the sash and keeps out the draught; but just think how hard it would be on the poor thing if it were to be made to stand upright, and pretend to be a poker."

"It couldn't; so your parallel does not lie."

"Oh! yes it could, if it were wrapped up tightly in stiff paper, but it would feel very uncomfortable."

"Well," and he laughed again, "you are not exactly wrapped up in paper to-night."

"Ah, no. To-night I am undisguised sand and red felt."

He had not intended to carry on her metaphor. He had thought from her change of tone that she was tired of her more serious mood, and had only meant to imply that she had a very pretty frock on, and looked very nice indeed. He had been coming steadily all this time to an emphatic opinion that

she was a very pretty girl, more than pretty—
she was strikingly handsome. He recollected that
when, some months before, they had first been
introduced, she had seemed to like him, and about
a month ago, when he had been told off to take her
down to dinner, she had been, as she had herself
just admitted, distinctly pleased. He was gratified
that such a girl should be glad to see him, and he
admired her for being frank enough to show it. He
sat looking at her brilliant colour, her long slender
hands, and her white throat, and thinking.

"Do you remember the last time we met?" he
asked suddenly.

"Yes, at dinner, at Mrs. Vallance's. You took
me in."

"Yes.   We had a very interesting conversation
together.   Not so interesting as this, but very
interesting.   Yet when you said good-night you
had changed, you were colder.   You gave me the
impression that I had vexed you.   Had I?"

"Yes," she said.

"Will you tell me how?   And forgive me?"

"I had rather forgive you without telling you."

"But I had rather be told.   Tell me, and then I
shan't do it again whatever it was.   You were
talking to me and Vallance in just the same
friendly way as you are talking to me now, and
suddenly you were vexed.   Why was it?"

"It was because when—someone else came up,
you and Mr. Vallance gave way at once, as if the
newcomer had some special right."

"He had a very special manner," O'Ruac said slowly, and looking at her searchingly.

"Ah, that is just what angered me," she cried impulsively. "You men consider each other so much and us so little. Let any man assume a certain air of appropriation with any girl, and all the rest of you will give way at his approach, till the girl feels that everyone is in a conspiracy against her—that she is being hurried along very much faster than she would go if left to herself; and it is most painful—especially if the girl is not sure she wants to go that road at all."

She stopped, blushing crimson, and very much ashamed of herself for having said so much ; telling herself that such frankness was almost indecent, and wondering if O'Ruac were as shocked as she was herself.

But he was not shocked at all. The average man is not apt to censure very severely the unconventionalities of a pretty woman who shows a marked liking for him. O'Ruac looking at Gertrude, and seeing nothing to disapprove of, misread her blush. "Ah, she is sure about the road now," he said to himself, and he was amazed to find that the thought gave him positive pain.

"Too late" has a bitter sound if said of the most trifling opportunity lost. We may sit debating lazily all the afternoon whether it be worth while to go on a certain expedition, until someone reminds us that it is "too late" to go, and we then immediately feel a regret quite out of proportion to our loss. We see in our minds all manner of pleasure and profit that might have been consequent on that expedition. We feel that a day created simply for that one purpose has been wasted.

O'Ruac stood thinking. Last time he had seen this girl it would not have been too late. She had not been sure then of the road she would choose, now she was sure of it. What had been possible then was not possible now. He was a good deal astonished to find himself actually suffering as he realised his lost chance. He was half angry with himself too. Surely he, as he had known himself until now, was not a man likely to give place to vague regrets, sentimental speculations as to what might have been. Suppose that a month ago something very beautiful had been within his reach and he had let it go by, was there any use in fretting like a child?

If a month ago there existed all the wonderful possibilities and limitless surprises of love between him and this woman, and now such possibilities existed no longer, the loss must be borne, as he had borne other troubles.

The loss of what had not been, but only might have been his, ought not to be too great for a man to bear; there were other women in the world.

Who has not at some time or other while wandering among country roads come for the first time on some old garden of a ruined manor house, and peering through the chinks of the big locked gate, caught tantalising glimpses of the delights within? The wild growing roses, all changed and grown pale like ghosts since that great gate was locked, the wonderful winding red clay paths, the quaint arbours, the half fallen trees—the dim statues, that might speak were we but near enough to hear, the broken fountains, and the quiet lawns, with such a sunset heaven of daffodils, a place of silence and mystery. Is there any garden in all the world, any *accessible* garden that can equal it? What makes the sunset within that locked gate so golden, when it has turned grey already in the road where we stand? Oh! those wonderful red pathways, to what do they lead? Oh, those silent statues! what would they tell us if we found out their language and spoke to them? Oh, that locked gate!

Well, such as are agile might climb over, such as are muscular might break the lock in the case of an actual garden, but O'Ruac stood outside a metaphorical locked gate, remembering that a month ago the key had not been turned.

Then he pushed all this sentimental nonsense out of his mind and tried to think of something commonplace to say, but for the first time within his memory, failed. Gertrude had risen, and they began to walk slowly down the long pathway towards the lights again; the girl had recovered her composure, and made some trivial good-natured remark about a pretty girl who passed.   Ashley came out of a marquee near at hand, and came towards them.

"Don't you think it about time you had some supper?" he said to Gertrude cheerfully, speaking before he quite reached her.

"I suppose, *now*, it will be right for me to give place?" O'Ruac said in a low tone.

"Yes.   Thank you; I should like some supper."

There was a slight pause between the first word and the second; as Gertrude and Ashley moved away, O'Ruac wondered whether that "yes" had been in answer to him, or if she had not heard his question, or having heard would not answer it.

The evening was about half over, and so far it was a distinct success.   O'Ruac was standing beside Lady Morley; they were watching the light frocks of the women appearing and disappearing among the trees; here and there the red ends of cigars were moving about in the darkness.   A brisk wind had sprung up, but it was a warm wind, and the night was all the pleasanter for it.

No one seemed to care to dance much, the band was playing valses languidly, but the night was still too warm for much exertion, almost everyone seemed to prefer to wander slowly among the lights and shadows.   As Lady Morley remarked, it must have been an exciting evening for anxious chaperons.

Gertrude and Ashley came out of the supper tent. She left him and joined a little group of girls who had gathered round an old sun dial, and were laughing with the easily raised laugh of health and good temper at the big cousin of one of the girls, who was courageously trying the very old joke of lighting a match to see what time it was. A few more cousins and brothers were standing near smoking, and wearing that look of tolerant superiority men generally assume when one of their number is so good-natured as to make a fool of himself for the amusement of the rest.

Presently, one energetic girl, fresh from school last term, began saying she wanted to dance, and that everyone was very lazy.

"Such a shame," she exclaimed, "why the lawn is so slippery you could almost skate on it, and the band is playing so deliciously."

"Oh, I'll dance with you, Mab, if you like," said the big cousin, with the air of making a great concession, "it won't be so bad, now this wind has sprung up. We shall have rain to-morrow, so we had better make the most of to-night ; come along."

He threw away his cigar, and they moved away together ; the rest laughed.

"These children from school have so much energy," said a girl who had left school at Christmas, and so of course was quite *blasee* by now, for she had been to the county ball and three dinner-parties, and had sung at the Sunday School Concert.

"Yes, time changes us all," said her brother,

gravely.   "Why it is quite a year now since you last gave me a black eye for letting your chickens out of the yard."

"Bevis, I didn't," cried the girl, dropping her "society tone" with startling abruptness.   "I didn't. I had a garden rake in my hand, and turned round suddenly, and you were in the way: that was all."

The little group went on laughing and chattering, one or two couples moved off in the direction of the band till none but girls were left; these still stood talking gaily of the events of the evening, till suddenly one of them cried out, "Look, Gertrude, Gertrude!   You are on fire."

So she was.   Either the match, dropped carelessly a few moments before, or a cigar-end flung away by someone going to dance, had set light to the dry grass, and the flame had crept along the ground before the wind.   It reached Gertrude's skirts and set them alight.

Gertrude looked down at her skirts.   True to her training her first instinct was to start away from beside the other girls, lest she should set them on fire too; but this brought her just into the full force of the wind, which, rising that moment in a sudden gust, caused the smouldering flame to leap up fiercely.

Then, realising that she was in great danger, she caught hold of her skirts, and tried to extinguish the flames with her hands.

Failing in this, she looked eagerly round for help.

Except the frightened girls standing helpless and useless with fear, no one seemed near. She cried out with all her strength, "Gilbert, Gilbert!" and then, with a last effort of self-control, threw herself on the ground, with her head towards the wind.

It was all over in a few moments. Gertrude was helped to her feet again and given some wine. She drank it, and handed the glass back to Gilbert with a smile.

"Thank you; I am all right, am I not?" and with natural feminine anxiety she passed her hand over face and hair to make sure she was not disfigured. "I am not hurt at all, I think?"

"You are not much hurt, thanks to your own presence of mind in throwing yourself on the ground as you did," said Gilbert, gravely.

"Thanks to you, you mean, for coming to help me so bravely. I am so proud of you, Gilbert."

Surely, it was almost brutality to be truthful at such a moment. Incomparably sweet as such words must have been for him to hear, they had been far sweeter for her to speak. If the men who love us delight in our praise, their pleasure in hearing is not to be compared with ours when they give us reason to praise them. Surely, at such a time, and before so many witnesses, Ashley might have been pardoned if he had kept silent, but he chose to speak.

"It was not I who did it, Trudie. It was not I who saved you, I was coming to do what I could, but O'Ruac was nearer, and—stronger. See my dear, I could not have done that."

He pointed as he spoke towards the nearest marquee, from which the great door curtain had been literally torn away with a force that had completely wrecked that end of the tent. The huge piece of striped canvas lay on the ground beside her, it was with that the flames had been extinguished so quickly.

He watched her eagerly. If she had reproached him, if she had spoken angrily, or even scornfully, he could have borne it, or if she had quarrelled with him finally then and there in unreasonable anger at what was no fault of his. He could have borne anything better than that she should lay her hand on his arm with a smile so openly tender, speak in a voice so markedly kind.

"Will you take me home, dear? I am not hurt in the least, but I should like you to take me home."

He knew what it meant—he knew too well what it meant. That she would hold to him not for love but for his sake. Not because his love was necessary to the completeness of her own life, but because his life would be strengthened by her loyalty. He saw that she realised how, married to him, her part all through their lives would be to support, and to strengthen him, and he saw that voluntarily and with open eyes she accepted her part—from kindness, not from love.

How strong she seemed to him, and how brave. All the bystanders must have seen her look, heard her tone; there was as much defiance of them as tenderness for him in it. She had almost said in reality what he had suggested in sport that she should say, " He is mine, let no one dare to blame him, or think slightingly of him."

It did not occur to him that he was absolutely undeserving of blame. It is no crime in a man not to be six feet high, and have the strength of a cart horse, and the agility of an Arab. The one thought in his mind was that another man had been before him in saving his betrothed from danger.

They had gone a few steps when Gertrude stopped short.

" I can't, I can't," she gasped. " I am hurt much more than I thought; I am horribly hurt, go for help, Gilbert."

By this time (the whole incident had not taken more than five minutes) the news had reached Lady Morley, she hurried up accompanied by a doctor who had been among the guests, and Gertrude was taken home and put to bed.

It was found that though she was not seriously injured, the wind having driven the flames towards her feet, her ankles and insteps were severely scorched, but not enough to threaten lameness or give rise to any anxiety.

The whole affair was not serious enough to interrupt the ball; it was merely a matter of a few days' pain. When Ashley had taken Gertrude home, the young people, after a few moments given to genuine regret and sympathy, resumed their enjoyment of the evening.

Only when O'Ruac was looked for to give an account of the rescue he could not be found anywhere.

CHAPTER III.

GILBERT ASHLEY.

ONE feels half ashamed of attending to the ordinary affairs of life in the shadow of a great calamity; they are so small that in the darkness we can scarcely see them. I remember when a child being startled and shocked to see a widow of a few hours, standing in the hall disputing with a market gardener over the price of strawberries; yet the friends who came from a distance, dusty and tired, were pleased to see those strawberries on the tea-table, and ate them with evident enjoyment.

Gertrude's injuries were no great calamity. She would be all right in the course of a week or two. She had already sent Ashley one or two kind little notes, that had somehow a distinctly "affianced" tone in them; but it is a terrible thing when the one we would have loving is only kind. That was the calamity, the revelation her words, her looks had made; and this calamity was so great that no remedy for it seemed possible.

All the same, when some of the servants told

Ashley that the new windows which he had had put into his library leaked, and were letting in the rain, which had been falling heavily for the last few days, he set out instantly to Churchhaven to see the contractor who had put them in. Not that in his present state of mind he would have cared much if the rain had flooded all the place, and swept his books, and his house, and himself into the bargain, off the face of the earth, but because under the circumstances to go and swear at the contractor was the natural and rational thing to do.

Churchhaven was at some distance, quite out of his own neighbourhood. He had gone there because he had heard that the Churchhaven builder had set up a remarkably fine greenhouse. When he got to Churchhaven he was beyond the little circle of his own neighbourhood, where he knew everyone, and everyone knew him.

It was raining heavily as he came out of the contractor's office, so he stopped to shelter under an archway leading into an inn yard. Two men in riding dress came out of the inn door, calling to the ostler not to bring out their horses until the shower was over.

The two men lounged against the doorway talking with that peculiar recklessness so many people indulge in in the presence of mere strangers. They were telling each other highly interesting stories of people Ashley only knew by name or did not know at all, so he scarcely heeded what he heard till one of them said:

" Yes, O'Ruac is a queer obstinate kind of fellow, but I am sorry he is going abroad."

" It's a sudden idea, isn't it ? "

" Sudden ? Oh, spasmodic. Why he was coming to stay with us when he left Valeshire ; he was staying with an aunt or something of the sort down there. Perhaps she's mad, and bit him ; anyhow he sent word he couldn't come to us, because he was going to the Cape."

" Didn't he give a reason ? "

" Well, business ; but he can't have any business at the Cape. Murphy asked him what it meant— Murphy is a great chum of his—he only laughed, and said there was a fire, and he'd been badly burnt, and wanted a change of air. I believe there was a fire of some sort, but one doesn't want a change of air for a burn ; if one did, there's plenty of air between this and Africa. Anyhow, whatever it means, he sails to-night in the *Hesperus*."

Ashley did not wait for the rain to stop after that. He hurried down to the telegraph office, and wired home to have a portmanteau packed and sent to him at London Bridge Station (Churchhaven being some three hours further from London than his own village), and then took the train to town.

He just caught the *Hesperus,* being the last passenger to go on board.

It was most undignified, and unromantic, but the steamer no sooner began to move than Ashley became deadly sea-sick. He inquired and found out that O'Ruac was really on board, and then went below. He devoted the first hour or two to wondering what he should say to O'Ruac, and how he should lead up to what he had to say. But after that nature was too strong for him, and he gave himself up to the tragic luxury of thinking that he was going to die, and wishing that he could do it quickly.

O'Ruac was not sea-sick. He had not even a "queer half hour." In spite of the fact that one hand was still tied up in cotton wool, and that his face was still red and sore from the scorching it had received—in spite, too, of that new trouble that was not to be conquered or cast off, strive as he might, he went about looking healthy and cheerful, and attacking breakfast, luncheon, tea and dinner with a vigour and energy that made the weaker passengers feel positively faint with envy.

It was over a week before Ashley managed to crawl on deck ; when he did so the clear air and the fresh wind soon began to make him feel quite himself again.   He was leaning against the rails when O'Ruac saw him, and came up.

" Hallo," he exclaimed in surprise, "you here ?"

" Hallo ! you here too ? " echoed Ashley as naturally as he could, for he had decided what line to take.

"Yes," said O'Ruac, "I thought I would travel a little, and you ? "

" I am going for good."

He spoke in a perfectly commonplace tone. O'Ruac said, "Oh," with an accent of intense surprise, and then, after a pause asked:

"How is Miss Southey?"

The words were merely conventional, but the tone asked a great deal.

"Miss Southey? Oh! I suppose she will be quite recovered by now. She was not much hurt, thanks to your promptitude, only rather frightened."

"Ashley—I wish—you speak as if—I should like to know——"

Was Gertrude's ideal of resolution actually hesitating and incoherent for the first time in his life? Yes, indeed, and his great, powerful hand was shaking visibly as he grasped the rail, his firm lips were as tremulous as a girl's.

Ashley was lazily making a cigarette, and giving all his attention to it.

"Have you quarrelled?" O'Ruac asked abruptly.

"Quarrelled? Oh! dear, no. Gertrude and I are far too good friends ever to quarrel. What should we quarrel about?"

"I had a sort of an idea, from your manner—and hers, that you and she were engaged."

"You were wrong, then," Ashley said, coolly. "We weren't. I believe we thought about it a little at one time, but we thought—it wouldn't do."

"You were not engaged that night, then?"

"No, we were never engaged."

"Ah!"

Still steadily refusing to see the other's emotion, Ashley looked out to sea.

"There is a home coming steamer," he said lazily, "we are going to stop. The captain told me so, he said it was against the rules in an ordinary way, but it is because of some important news someone connected with the company who is on board with us expects from Port Said. Anyone who likes will be able to send letters home."

"Well," O'Ruac said slowly, "I must go, if there is a chance of sending letters home. I must write one."

"Must you?" said Ashley, indifferently, " so must I, but I need not hurry, mine is only a short one."

He stood, with his cigarette unlighted, looking straight out in front, while O'Ruac hurried below.

.　　.　　.　　.　　.　　.　　.　　.　　.

Gertrude had quite recovered from the injuries and the shock she had undergone. She was walking slowly up and down a gravel path in the garden, thinking.

The rains were over, and the weather was bright and warm again; the lawn was still soft and fresh with the showers of the last week, but the gravel path, and the old bench at the end of it were quite dry. Gertrude sat down when she came to the bench, and leaned back against the soft privet hedge, thinking still.

Had she done well? Well for herself and her

lover that night? Was it just to him to marry him only because he needed her, not because she wanted him? Was it just to herself to have accepted a life in which she must needs assume a leadership and mastership to which she knew herself to be by nature unequal, only because she knew her lover to be still more unequal to them?

That night a passion of tenderness for her lover's humiliation had prompted the course she had taken. She knew it had been a generous course, but had it been a wise or just one?

Had anyone, man or woman, a right to dare to marry another from any motive whatsoever, no matter how exalted and unselfish, but love?

"'I did it for his sake'"—"'I did it to save my family from ruin'"—"'Because I feared to break her heart, or because the disappointment might have wrecked his life if I had not.'" Idle reasons, idle reasons, one and all. Marriage is the death or life of the soul, and nothing less than perfect love can justify the awful risk of it.

And was not the fact that she could reason so logically, doubt so coherently, in itself a proof that she did not love Gilbert? His gentleness, his patience, his truth were all wonderfully pleasant to her, but did she love him? And what was more important, did he love her? Was she to make this great effort for the sake of a mere liking? Was there force and stamina in his easy-going nature for an eternal love ?　　And if not, what a waste of two lives.

He had said that he loved her.　If she could but believe it ; if she could but be sure ; if there were any proof of it possible !

She leaned back in her seat, her hands locked one within the other ; the postman was coming down the road, and stopped on the other side of the hedge.

" Two letters for you, miss."

She took them listlessly, and more to save the old man the long walk up the drive, than from any curiosity as to their contents.

Presently she saw that one of the letters was directed in Ashley's handwriting, and turning from it quickly, she saw that the other was in a strange hand.　She opened that letter first and looked at the signature.

" Owen O'Ruac."

Her face paled, her hand trembled, she held the letter out of her sight for a moment, as if afraid to read it: then she slowly raised it again, turned to the first page, and read.

The letter began formally, with " Dear Miss Southey," and was carefully written for the first line or two, but after that it seemed as if the writer's self-restraint gave way, and he wrote without reserve, straight from his heart to hers.　He told her how her supposed admission that she was betrothed to Gilbert Ashley had been a blow to him—a blow so great that its greatness had amazed and stunned him, how later, after that moment's pleasure of saving her from danger, he had learned that the blow was so heavy that he dared not trust himself to bear it in her presence.

"I know I am stubborn and self-willed," he went on. "I have all those vices whose virtuous counterparts you in your kindly judgment were so good as to praise in me; but I am not a brigand, I would not carry off another man's wife, I would not wish even to try to do so. That was my reason for leaving suddenly as I did. I could not have seen you and not spoken. I could not have remained in your neighbourhood and not tried to see you. It would have been distinctly wrong, you would have been angry, distressed, contemptuous; but none of these considerations would have stayed me.

"This very instant I learned from Ashley, first from the fact he is going to the Cape for good, then from his very frank and courteous answers to my questions, that I was mistaken. I had misunderstood you, you had not been engaged at all, that your love was not his—might perhaps be mine, or at any rate that the trial was free to me as to any other.

"I am coming home to try—to succeed unless I have misread you twice; unless such love as mine has no power to touch you. I shall leave the steamer at Port Said: wire to me there if I may come to you.   I shall come whether you give me leave or not, but bid me come all the same, my Gertrude; expect me, weary for me a little and love me when I come.

"OWEN O'RUAC."

Very slowly Gertrude opened the other letter, Gilbert Ashley's; it was soon read, for it contained but three words :—

"Believe it now."

ZAHNAHA'S LOVER.

ZAHNAHA'S LOVER.

"ZAHNAHA! open the door!"

The wind and the rain were crying all around the hut. Zahnaha, half asleep, drew the red-dyed goatskin close up to her ears. The light from the last sparks from the fire on the hearth shone on her lips. She smiled a little; it was so pleasant to be young and beautiful—and she was very beautiful. More beautiful than Mouska. Mouska's lips were like rubies, and her cheeks like the inside of the strange shells that travellers brought from the seas across the great plains eastward and westward; but Zahnaha's cheeks were like roses, and her lips like very red roses. Mouska's hair was like the twisted brass on the gates of the great cities of the north, and her arms like the smooth polished ivory on the spearshafts of the warriors who came over the mountains from the south; but Zahnaha's hair was like the fine gold silk the weavers stretch across their looms, and her arms were round and white and soft as the breast of a dove. The old folks said, and the young ones believed them, that some day a strange beautiful bridegroom would come to the village and choose out from among the girls the fairest for his bride, and who could say what would happen then?

"Zahnaha! open the door!"

It was as if the storm had taken voice and spoken. Still half asleep, she heard the hissing of the big drops of rain as they fell down the chimney on to the last sparks of the fire. She heard the wild cries and unearthly footsteps of the storm—and who knows of what else? Who knows what evil things crossed the great plain to-night, or rose from the mists of the long stagnant pools? Yet Zahnaha did not fear, for across the door was a branch of the holy tree, and Zahnaha was brave and kind. In her heart she pitied all the terrible things for which men must not pray—all the sad and lonely spirits doomed to unhuman immortality. "I wish God would give rest to them all," she sighed.

"Zahnaha! open the door!"

The cry of the storm crept in under the threshold, or was it an evil spirit, or a man's voice faint and weak, and imploring? It went to Zahnaha's heart; she rose, and, binding her girdle round her loosened robe, crept to the door, but she did not unfasten the latch.

"Who is there?" she cried. "Speak!" but she forgot to add, "in the name of God."

"I am here, Zahnaha, and I am weary with the storm, and wounded, and sick; for pity of me open the door, and let me rest by your fire."

"How can I dare to open the door?" said Zahnaha. "How do I know what evil thing you are, come across the great plains, or out of the long pools? Such a night as this is full of evil spirits."

"Alas! Zahnaha; no spirit could suffer as I do; open the door and succour me."

She laid her hand on the latch.

"But though you are a man, and not a spirit, how can I dare open the door? I am a girl, and alone; my hut is on the very edge of the village, and it is night; I must not open the door."

"Alas! Zahnaha, how could I harm you? You might crush me with your foot. Open the door and see."

"But how can I dare open the door? Though you are no spirit, nor cannot hurt me, when the door is opened to the storm evil things from the waste come in."

"But you need only open the door such a little way for me, Zahnaha. Open it a little, and see."

Zahnaha opened the door a very little way, and something crept in over the threshold. Zahnaha never noticed how the leaves of the branch of the holy tree all turned white and shivered, and crumpled themselves together as it passed. Was it a man? It seemed more like some withered, dying worm; no more a man than the broken, blighted stalk is corn; no more than the crushed chrysalis is a perfect moth; but it looked at her with the eyes of a man, and spoke to her with a man's voice.

"Your hut is warm, Zahnaha, and your face is fair, and your hands are strong; help me."

"What can I do to help you?" she said.

"I have a wound here—right on my heart," he said. "An enchantress did it; it has made me as you see, and I shall never be whole unless you heal me."

She was a little frightened, but she knelt by the fire. There was only one red spark left. She blew it into a blaze, and heaped on wood, and brought red-dyed skins for the thing to rest on, and sat down beside him. When the fire burnt up, and she saw plainly his dreadful misshapen form and sad eyes, her heart was full of pity for him.

"What can I do to heal you?" she said.

"You must bind my wound with your hair."

She unloosened her long hair, and wound it round his body, and presently she began to feel all the pain of his wound on her own heart.

"Ah, me," she sobbed, pitying him, "does a wounded heart give pain like this?"

"I suffer less, Zahnaha," he said, and indeed his voice was stronger and less sad. He seemed growing, too, for the bands of hair tightened. It was as if all her hairs were being drawn one by one from her head. The pain was dreadful; but for pity of him she did not complain or cry out any more; and at dawn, when he left her, he could go on his feet.

And at full day, when all the girls of the village went to draw water, they found a little ugly, crippled, and deformed old man sitting on the wall of the well. They all greeted him mockingly because he was so ill-favoured, and they asked him whence he had come, and if he had heard on his travels of the beautiful bridegroom, who one day was to come to the village, and the little deformed cripple answered them feebly and sullenly, "Who can tell where he is, or when he will come?"

Zahnaha was there, too, but she asked no questions, only smiled a little as she passed by with her full pitcher, and the other girls looked after her, and laughed lightly.

"There goes beautiful Zahnaha. Why does she speak to none of us this morning? How slowly she walks, and why does she wear that great ugly cap on her head?"

.   .   .   .

"Zahnaha! open the door!"

Zahnaha rose without a word, and opened the door. The little ugly cripple stood on the threshold.　She smiled without speaking, and led him in quickly, never noticing how all the leaves of the holy tree fell on the floor in a shower.　She made up the fire quickly, and placed seats, and sat beside him.

"Ah, Zahnaha," he said, "I am very wretched."

"What can I do?" said Zahnaha.　"Are you not healed of your wound?"

"Yes; but I am weak and deformed, and a cripple, and they mocked me in the village by the well; but you are strong and full of life, and if you would let me hold your hand for an hour I think that would do me good."

She hesitated a moment, but she gave him her hand.　It was as if her life flowed into him.　She could not forbear to cry out: "Let go! Let go! I shall die."　But it seemed as if he did not hear her, and presently she was glad he did not, for she fancied his pulse was growing stronger, and the very touch of his hand firmer every moment, so she let him keep his hold still, for pity of him.　The firelight grew dim in the hut, and the grey mist from the plains crept in under the threshold, and her eyes were weary, so she could not see very distinctly, but she fancied he grew tall and straight and strong, till at sunrise, when he left her, he was a hale man, but old and very ugly.

And at full day, when all the girls of the village came to draw water, and found the man sitting on the edge of the well, they asked him if he could tell them when the beautiful bridegroom was coming, and he answered in a strong voice, but harsh and rough, "Who knows; perhaps to-morrow."

And they wondered, and asked each other if this could be the little cripple they had seen yesterday morning. "How strange," they said, "how we were mistaken; he is not lame at all, only rough and ugly and old."

And Zahnaha said nothing, but passed by heavily with her full pitcher, and the girls looked after her, chattering to each other.

"How pale Zahnaha is to-day," they said; "how heavy her step is; she is less beautiful than we thought."

.   .   .   .

"Zahnaha, open the door."

"She was waiting for him, and threw the door open wide; never noticing how the bare bough of the holy tree had snapt in two and fell on the ground.

He flung himself upon the cushions of skin and sighed.

"Ah, Zahnaha! I am very sad," he said.

"What is left for me to do?" she answered.

"Zahnaha! Zahnaha! You are so young, so beautiful, you have done so much for me, do not grudge me this last kindness."

She trembled a little, but she answered pitifully:—

"I grudge you nothing that can help you."

"Then kiss me, Zahnaha."

And for pity of him she bent forward and put her lips to his.

It seemed as if she could never draw them away again. Something horrible was happening. His lips were like a knife piercing her lips; it was as if all the blood in her heart was flowing into his heart. She could not speak nor cry out, nor groan, because of his lips on hers. She grew weaker and weaker; but all the time she grudged him nothing.

Next morning was fine and bright. When all the girls came to draw water, they found a stranger sitting on the wall of the well, and they asked him who he was, and had he any news of the beautiful bridegroom, and he laughed aloud, and said, "Do you not know that I am he?"

And they looked, and saw that his face was very beautiful, and his body strong and straight, and he had gold armour on his breast, and gold rings on his hands. Then they all cried out joyfully, "It is he!—it is he, the bridegroom! See his beauty, and his height, and his lordly air! Let us hasten and put on our holiday dresses, and meet in the village for him to choose one of us. It is he for whom we have waited—the beautiful bridegroom!"

They forgot to wonder what had become of the rough man and the cripple.

Zahnaha had not gone to the well that morning, but in her hut she heard the shouting and tumult in the village, and knew what it meant. She rose wearily, and took her embroidered robe and gold girdle from the cedarwood chest, and covered her bare head with a veil, and went out into the village.

All the girls were there in their holiday dresses. The beautiful bridegroom walked about among them, and when he looked at any girl she seemed to grow taller and fairer for very pride. When he came to Mouska he stood still.

Nearly all the girls called out, "It is she ; he has chosen well. Mouska is fairer than any of us." But one or two said, "No ; let him wait till he has seen Zahnaha," and just then Zahnaha came and stood beside Mouska.

Mouska's cheeks were like pink sea shells, and her lips red like rubies, her hair like wrought brass, and her arms white and smooth like ivory ; and when the girls looked at her and Zahnaha standing together, they all cried out, "Mouska is the most beautiful. Why Zahnaha is not beautiful at all; see how pale she is, and haggard—like an old woman. Her arms are withered like berries in winter. And what has become of her hair? The bridegroom must choose Mouska "

"Let him choose for himself," said Zahnaha.

He just glanced carelessly at Zahnaha, and took Mouska by the hand and kissed her, and all the girls cried out, "Joy to the bride and bridegroom!"

Zahnaha crept away to her hut, old, and bent, and decrepit. No one but she had noticed that there was blood on the bridegroom's lips.

LADY ATHERTON'S SACHET.

Lady Atherton's Sachet.

"IT is not ready yet, Grédel," said Lady Atherton, looking up a moment from her work as her maid entered, "it surely can't be post-time."

" No, my lady, not for half an hour."

" I can't see anyone, if that's what you want," laughed Lady Atherton. "Colonel Brereton has interrupted me enough for one day."

" It is Mr. Durthwaite, my lady."

" Oh, well, I will see him, of course."

Grédel had expected that answer, for she had heard Sir Theodore Atherton tell his wife that Durthwaite was a good fellow, and clever, who might be useful, and ought to be educated ; and she knew that Lady Atherton had undertaken the task.

Mr. Nicolas Durthwaite was an attractive subject for education.   He was a very fine specimen of the genus—" Conservative Working Man "—and was the more interesting because he came from a part of the country where the soil is too barren for Conservatism to thrive well as a rule.

He was born a peasant in the wildest of the Cumberland wilds. Being considered a "parlish" clever fellow by his parents, they had been at some pains to give him a year or two of extra schooling beyond the requirements of the Board. Lately, on the death of a local squireen, to whom, in common with half the rest of the village, he was distantly related, he had inherited a moderate-sized estate; and he had just been elected a member of Parliament for his native place. He was a well-grown, frank-faced young man, with no self-consciousness, a good deal of self-content, and a sort of rustic directness of address. Sir Theodore said it was as healthy as a day's grouse shooting to talk to him.

"I can't talk to you just now," said Lady Atherton, as he entered, "I am very busy, as you see. I don't think you ever saw me so busy before."

"What is it?" he asked, looking in a bewilderment of admiration at the mysterious creation of silk and cord and lace in Lady Atherton's hands.

"A sachet. A thing to keep handkerchiefs in, you know. I shall have finished it soon, and shall be ready to talk to you or listen, whichever you like best. At present I must give all my energies to my work, as it must go by this post. It is a contribution to a charity bazaar."

Mr Durthwaite ejaculated, "Just think of that, now!" and sat down to think of it at his leisure.

He thought he had never in the world seen

anything quite so beautiful as Lady Atherton's long, graceful, white fingers flying about among the delicate fragments of lace and silk, and converting them into something so exquisitely fine he hadn't known the name of it. It was to him a wonderful and incomprehensible thing that he should have come all the way from the Cumberland moors, and be there in the drawing-room of his political leader, watching his leader's incomparable wife as she sewed.

He did not exactly know what he was there for. If anyone had told him he was being educated he would not have known enough to understand what was meant, and would probably have asked if that sort of thing wasn't generally done at school.

"There! it's finished," said Lady Atherton. "What do you think of it?"

It was certainly a very creditable piece of fancy work as such things go. The beginning of it had apparently been a big piece of pale lemon-coloured silk, painted all over with great sleepy-looking lilies; and it was being sewn up into such a complication of lace and quilted satin and silk cord, that no mere man, much less poor rustic Nick, could have been expected to guess what its use might be.

"It's wonderful," he said, "just wonderful; but where do you put them?"

"The handkerchiefs? Why, here," and she pushed her slim blue-veined hand into two unexpected pockets, shaking out a faint perfume as she did so.

R

Nick's mind flew back to the terrible square yards of red cotton of his youth. At that moment he felt very much educated, if he had only known it.

"It's just wonderful!" repeated Nick; "and did you really invent all that yourself?"

"Oh dear, no. I have not imagination enough to invent anything. It is an exact copy of one of my wedding presents. The giver, a great friend of mind, did design it. I think you know her, Miss Haydon."

"Miss Haydon!" exclaimed Mr. Durthwaite, "isn't that the girl there is some story about?"

"My dear Mr. Durthwaite," said Lady Atherton sweetly, "there is never any story about a lady whom another lady mentions to you."

"I beg your pardon," said Nick promptly, "I won't say such a thing again."

"Don't. And now, please, tell me the story."

"Well, I heard that she jilted some poor man very abominably for the sake of some rich one."

"Please contradict that story on my authority if you hear it again."

"Certainly. Isn't it true, then?"

"Oh, if it were true it would have been contradicted long ago. I know nothing about it, but I shall ask Miss Haydon. Meanwhile, I know my friend. Will you ring, please?"

"You can take this now, Grédel," said Lady Atherton, as her maid entered. "You will find the packet of autographs in my handkerchief-case. Put them with this and direct it to ' Mrs. Easterhouse, The Town Hall, Clayton.' She might miss it if it were sent to her house."

" It is convenient sometimes to be the wife of a politician," said Lady Atherton, turning to Nick ; " one can contribute to a bazaar so easily. Mrs. Easterhouse tells me the good Tories of Clayton will give as much as half-a-crown for one of Teddy's autographs."

" Of course. I once gave seven-and-sixpence for one of Lord Beaconsfield's, and when money was very scarce with me, too. It's very good of Sir Theodore to write them."

" He doesn't," laughed Lady Atherton ; " no earthly power could induce him to write an autograph. I have been cutting these off his old letters. It was very generous of me, don't you think ? "

Lady Atherton might have added that she had had great difficulty in finding a sufficient number of autographs of Sir Theodore Atherton which were suitable for publicity, most of the letters of that eminent statesman being signed, " Till death, your loving Teddy." And though such signatures would undoubtedly have brought a much higher price than the more conventional, " Yours ever, T. H. Atherton," there were limits to her generosity.

Nick was seized with a bright idea.

" Why, I can be as generous as you," he said, " if a bazaar ever comes my way. I have a lot of letters from you."

"Notes, you mean; but I am afraid they would be of no use. You see, I am nobody; I am only somebody's wife. Besides, no one would ever be sure mine was genuine; I write differently every time I take a new pen. Teddy says whenever he receives a letter in a strange hand he expects to find it is from me."

Nick could never get quite used to hearing his political leader spoken of as " Teddy."   It was all very well of Lady Atherton to say it, but he felt almost presumptuous in hearing it said. People who live in town, and can see their favourite heroes and prophets every day, can ride on the same bus with them, or patronise the same butcher, cannot ever be brought to understand the intense veneration the dwellers on the borders and outskirts of civilisation feel for the leaders and movers of society and of the political world.

A good many people had taken young Durthwaite up; partly, perhaps, on account of the strong liking Sir Theodore Atherton had conceived for him, but more because they found his frank, easy-going country innocence wonderfully attractive.   Nick was at first utterly bewildered when he found himself associating with people who until now had only been to him the great names that made the newspapers interesting; but now he was beginning to take things as they came, and to enjoy them very much, but most of all he enjoyed being educated by Lady Atherton.

Sir Theodore was not the leader of his party, but he was one of them, and had always been Nick's hero and prophet, even when he, too, had been only a name in the newspapers. Nick worshipped him more enthusiastically than ever now he knew him as a friend and a host, possessed of a real personality and a beautiful wife.

It was not very long since Nick had given so much more than he could afford for Lord Beaconsfield's signature, and all through the remainder of his conversation with Lady Atherton that afternoon he was forming a wild, romantic resolve. Lady Atherton had said that wonderful piece of work was for a charity bazaar. Anyone could buy it who liked, of course, and why not he as well as another? He had heard the address, he knew where it was going. Let the Clayton Tories content themselves with the autographs. The work would be no precious relic to them, Lady Atherton had said so. It would be only a—a—well, he didn't exactly remember what, but a thing to put handkerchiefs in; but to him it was almost sacred. When he left Lady Atherton's drawing-room he went straight to the nearest railway station to get a time table and find out where Clayton was. It was a good deal farther off than he had expected, but he found that if he took a late train that night he should reach Clayton almost as soon as the bazaar was opened, and then, having secured the sachet, get back to town in time to dress for dinner.

Sir Theodore Atherton was more than a great politician—he was a good husband, though, perhaps, rather a dull one. At home he was a quiet, indolent man, whose share in domestic discussions consisted generally of sitting with his chin on his hands hearing his wife talk, and interjecting "yes," whenever she paused. Sometimes, indeed, he would achieve a longer sentence, but it was always with a very apparent effort, and gave one the impression that he had forgotten the language, or had exhausted all his store of complete sentences last debate, and was searching the odd nooks and corners of his memory for any fragment that might be left.

Lady Atherton complained sometimes that if ever she wanted to hear her husband talk she had to go to the House of Commons; but, on the whole, she was contented with him, and he, on his part, was most completely contented with her.

During dinner on the evening of Mr. Durthwaite's visit, Lady Atherton began to give her husband details as to his education.

"I think we may call him nearly finished now, Teddy," she said. "Do you know what we must do next?"

Sir Theodore said "Yes," not at all in answer to the question, but to signify that he was ready to receive another idea.

"When we have finished educating him we must marry him!"

Sir Theodore slowly changed the hand that was

supporting his chin, and said, "Why not?" Then, as an after thought, "Who?"

"What do you think of Kate Haydon?"

"Oh, dear, no!" said Sir Theodore, startled into emphasis. "She's the girl who behaved so badly to Brereton."

"You never told me anyone had behaved badly, as you call it, to Colonel Brereton."

"Didn't I? He tells me often enough."

"Well, Kate never even mentioned Colonel Brereton's name to me."

"Yes," said Sir Theodore, leaving the conversation with her.

"Teddy," said his wife sternly, "I am, as you know, the most open-hearted, confiding young woman on all the face of the earth. I tell you everything I know on every subject with the most unlimited generosity, whether you are interested or not; but you, and Colonel Brereton, and Kate Haydon, who are all my nearest friends, are the most abominably reticent set of people existent. This is the second time I have heard hints of a dark and tragic secret between two of you. Be so good as to collect your faculties and tell me every word of the story."

Atherton felt himself in for it, so he leaned forward a little more, and began resignedly:—

"Well, she was engaged to Brereton, or perhaps she wasn't quite engaged, and another fellow, awfully rich, turned up, and Brereton was jealous.

And she did not write to him, and got engaged to the other fellow; but he died, so she wasn't married."

"Was there any special reason why she should write to him?"

"I can't say.   That's all I know; and it has just spoilt Brereton."

"I shall ask her about it, Teddy.   She ought to have told me.   Not all that, of course; for I don't believe half of it is true, but her version."

"I only wish Brereton wouldn't tell me; so often, I mean.   He can talk of nothing else—no, nothing else except her, but all women.   Doesn't believe in them; thinks they're no good, that sort of thing. It's awfully tedious."

"Oh, Teddy, I should never have thought it.   I always found him so attentive—and fatherly almost. I am sure he likes me."

If Atherton had spoken what was in his mind, he would have said, "Brereton thinks just well enough of you to think you worth watching, and I, who think a woman who wanted watching would be worth nothing, am on the verge of quarrelling with him on this account;" but he didn't.   He only said that Brereton was a lunatic, and then added, after a moment or two, "But he's a good fellow, and I've got into the habit of being very fond of him."

"Poor Colonel Brereton!   I am very sorry for him," said Lady Atherton.   And she continued to be sorry for him at intervals all the evening, and began to wonder if it would not be a better plan to reconcile Colonel Brereton to Miss Haydon than to marry her to Mr. Durthwaite.

Mr. Durthwaite arrived at Clayton Town Hall a few moments after the bazaar was opened, and lost no time in enquiring for Mrs. Easterhouse's stall.

"You are our first customer," said that lady pleasantly, "I must show you something very pretty."

"You are very good. I want something to put handkerchiefs in," he said.

"Anything of this sort?" showing him several very serviceable-looking carved wooden boxes.

"Oh, no, not at all. It must be made of silk and lace, and be pretty, very pretty."

"Oh, indeed!" and concluding that this very good-looking young man wanted to choose a present for a lady, Mrs. Easterhouse began to take an interest in him, and showed him every handkerchief sachet on her stall, but in vain.

At last, when she had began to lose patience, a pretty girl came forward and handed her a packet.

"This has just come by post, mother," she said. "I suppose it is Lady Atherton's handkerchief sachet."

"Now," said Mrs. Easterhouse, turning to Nick as she opened it, "if this does not satisfy you I give up in despair. Look, is it not beautiful?"

"Oh," exclaimed Nick, trying to smother his delight, "that might do, now."

But Mrs. Easterhouse was too quick for him. She had seen the start of recognition, and, mistaking it for admiration, she nearly doubled the price of the sachet in consequence. She overcharged him abominably, in fact, but he neither knew nor cared. He had got it at last, that was all he cared about. He bore it away in triumph, and rejoiced over it all the way home.

It was just beginning to rain when Nick reached his rooms. He hurried in and changed quickly, because he had promised himself an exquisite pleasure afterwards. Not knowing that a sachet was purely a lady's luxury, he thought it would be a most delightful thing to keep his own handkerchiefs in a case of Lady Atherton's workmanship, to let his ordinary, commonplace linen be idealised and poeticised by resting in the fragrant, fascinating pocket where her gracious hands had wandered.

Now Colonel Brereton, walking towards his club, had been caught in the rain, and it occurred to him to call at Durthwaite's and borrow an umbrella. Durthwaite, of course, did not expect any visitor at that hour, and when his landlady announced, "Colonel Brereton, to borrow an umbrella," he had just taken the sachet from the papers it had travelled in, and in which Mrs. Easterhouse had repacked it, and had begun to arrange some of his handkerchiefs in it. He felt a little awkward at being discovered so occupied. Brereton started, and looked pointedly at the sachet.

" What have you got there ? " he said.

" It's a sachet," said Nick, who had got the name by heart now.

" So I see," said Brereton.

" I bought it at a bazaar," said Nick awkwardly, vaguely conscious of something disagreeable in the other's manner.

" Oh, indeed ! " said Brereton, looking intently at the marked postage stamp on the wrapper.

Nick felt his hand, still in one of the pockets, touch on something hard. He started perceptibly, and drew out his hand, displacing as he did so a sealed envelope, which fell on the floor.

" Oh," said Colonel Brereton drily, " did you buy that at the bazaar, too ? "

" Wherever I bought it it concerns me, not you," said Nick angrily. He picked up the envelope, opened it, and read the contents slowly and deliberately. When he had finished, Brereton was still watching him.

" You came for an umbrella, I think ? " said Nick quietly.

" Yes, but it has stopped raining."

It was pouring in torrents, but Colonel Brereton did not feel like borrowing an umbrella. He was dreadfully angry. He called a hansom, and drove to Sir Theodore Atherton's ; he found Sir Theodore stretched at full length on his dressing-room sofa, doing nothing.

" I wish to goodness you wouldn't lay yourself

out like that," said Brereton fretfully, "you only want a sheet to give one the idea you're dead."

"Since you always make as much noise coming in as the Judgment Day, it doesn't much matter," said Sir Theodore, half opening his eyes. "You hav'n't come to dinner?" he added, with a shade of anxiety in his voice.

"No; that's to-morrow."

"Wouldn't come if I were you. Wouldn't myself if I wasn't obliged. Thought it *was* to-morrow—dinner-day, I mean—for a moment;" but settling his mind to rest again, "Muriel would have reminded me sooner."

"Look here, Atherton," said his friend, "I have something to say to you."

"Oh, well, sit down somewhere," then, as an after thought, "and begin."

But Brereton found it a hard matter to begin. "Look here, Atherton," he said, "I have told you often you don't take enough care of your wife."

"Yes," said Atherton patiently, "are you going to tell me so again?"

"I have told you often how unwise it is to allow Lady Atherton to associate with Miss Haydon. There is no limit to the harm one false woman can do."

"To another false woman," said Atherton, coldly. But Brereton was too full of his own thoughts to note Atherton's meaning.

"I don't want to say more than I need, but there

are some things you ought to know ; for instance, how often young Durthwaite comes here."

"Mr. Durthwaite comes at my desire, and it's awfully good of Lady Atherton to take so much trouble about him."

"Atherton," said his friend, "do you suppose I like speaking in this way?   Can I have any motive except to serve you ?"

"There's a story my wife tells," began Atherton, slowly, "at least, I don't think she ever told it to any one except me, but I daresay she wouldn't mind if I repeated it just now.   She says it's the only time she ever sympathised in swearing.   It's about an Irishman.   That's not important, but the fellow was Irish, and she—Muriel, you know—says the story is so pretty she must give the credit where it belongs.

"She was staying at a little seaport town where steamers used to start for Belfast.   The steamer was supposed to wait for the mid-day train, only nobody ever came by it, so the steamer people were a trifle careless.

"Well, one day Muriel was down at the pier. The steamer was a little quicker than usual, and just passed the dock-gates as the train drew up, and for a wonder there was one passenger, who, of course, never supposing but that the steamer would wait for the train, came down along the platform at a good easy pace to where the steamer was quietly moving alongside the pier.   He kept up with it, expecting every moment that it would stop against the pier to take up passengers; but gradually it dawned upon him that the passengers were already on board, that the steamer was getting up steam, and widening the distance between itself and the pier; that, in fact, the steamer had started. Well, he took a fresh grip on his valise, stepped backward to the farther side of the pier, made a mental calculation of the distance, and aiming some eight feet behind where he wanted to alight to allow for the speed of the steamer, ran.   Muriel, who always went in for athletics, said she expected to see a remarkably fine jump, but at the last moment someone in the crowd threw his arms round the Irishman, explaining volubly that it was impossible, he couldn't do it, he would have been drowned.

"It was impossible, thanks to that interference; a moment before it wouldn't have been.   The Irishman saw this as he looked at the now hopelessly distant steamer, then he turned, Muriel says, with a sort of patient exasperation, at the other fellow and said:

"'I am much obliged to you, sir, for your damned officiousness.'"

"Atherton," cried Brereton reproachfully, "is that for me?   Is it quarrelling?"

"It has come to that," said the other, rising suddenly, and speaking with quiet energy.   "Muriel must not be discussed.   Muriel must not be criticised. I am very sorry for the way Miss Haydon behaved to you, and I can understand how that has made you suspicious, though I am beginning to fancy you are in error there; but in any case Muriel is not to be judged by Miss Haydon's standard. I've known you all my life, Brereton, and I like you better than any man I know, and I've borne with your nonsense a long time; but understand now finally, I will never again hear one word of criticism concerning Muriel Summers."

It was characteristic of the man that he spoke of his wife by her maiden name, under which he had first known and believed in her. That "Cæsar's wife" must be above suspicion, is, after all, but an expression of marital vanity. This was a demand for faith in the desire of the individual truth of one woman.

Brereton was astounded. He did not remember to have ever heard his friend speak so earnestly, and so completely (in private life, that is) since they had been at Eton together, but he was so thoroughly convinced of the falseness of all women, even including Lady Atherton, that he felt he must speak.

"Please yourself," he said. "I think any man in the world but I would leave you to your fate after that, but if you don't hear what I have to say now, other people will say worse things soon, that you may not have a chance of hearing till too late. I have just left Durthwaite admiring and fondling an elaborate piece of what women call fancy work, which I saw your wife sewing at the day before yesterday!"

"He is welcome to anything Lady Atherton chooses to send him."

"Then why need he tell me he bought it, or look so annoyed when I saw there was a letter sent with it?"

"She may send letters on any and every subject she likes, to any and everyone she chooses."

"Atherton, this makes it all the worse of her, when you believe in her like that. He didn't expect that letter. It was sent in the other thing, and took him quite by surprise. He flushed like a girl. He could scarcely speak when he wanted to send me off. It was a shame to watch him. Atherton, I am horribly shocked and grieved about this. It's terrible. But I had to tell you."

Atherton looked at him slowly and considered.

"You are a good fellow after all, Tommy," he said. "Ring for a cab, will you? while I put some boots on. I want to be quick."

"What are you going to do?" said Brereton anxiously.

"Oh, we'll go round to Durthwaite's, don't you think? and hear about it."

.   .   .   .

Brereton had given a perfectly true description of Mr. Durthwaite's emotions when he read the contents of that unlucky envelope, for the poor fellow had been more shocked and amazed than he had ever been before in his life. He had expected the envelope to contain only some few of Sir Theodore's autographs left in the sachet by mistake, but this was what he read :—

" Are you acting honestly by me, or kindly? You behave as if you loved me, and yet you do not speak. What can I do? You know I am not free, and I am not strong nor brave. I know you are proud, but don't let your pride make you cruel. I know you love me, but I want your word for it. Only speak, and then neither my bondage to others, nor the opinion of the world, nor any other consideration shall keep me from you."

Now when Nick had read this and got rid of Colonel Brereton, he sat down by the fire to think of it, and he thought it was the most terrible thing that had ever happened to him, or ever could have happened.

It did not occur to him to wonder whether the letter was meant for him or for another, or to speculate as to how it came to be in such a place ; the thing was that Lady Atherton had written it, and the thought was appalling.

Why, if she had written it she was wicked, downright wicked ; and Sir Theodore must be a fool, not to have found that out. And if that were so, if his sweet, grand, gracious empress were deceiving her husband, if his prophet and leader were not astute enough to know truth from falsehood, why, there was an end of everything as far as he could see, and life generally speaking was a failure.
                                                        S

And what if the letter were for him? What if Lady Atherton with her wonderful cleverness, had somehow known what he would do, had seen as she so often did what was passing in his mind, had put the letter in the sachet on purpose for him, had actually incited him to act disloyally to his own chosen chief and oracle? The thought was frightful. He sat before the fire with the letter in his hands, about the most miserable, perplexed, ashamed young man in the universe.

Sir Theodore and Colonel Brereton found him so when they entered. He started to his feet, thrusting the letter as he did so into his pocket.

"We're disturbing you, I fear," said Sir Theodore, "we won't keep you long."

Nick looked up and noticed for the first time that his dinner had been served while he was studying the letter. He wondered how Sir Theodore could think of such a trifle, or be ready with any conventional phrase. He made none. It never occurred to him his visitors would expect it. The letter filled the whole universe for him.

Seeing his miserable embarrassment, a faint look of surprise came into Sir Theodore's eyes; but he went on with the sentences he had evidently prepared on his way.

"Colonel Brereton has got an absurd idea," he began; "he does get absurd ideas sometimes, but he's a good fellow, so I can't quarrel with him as I ought, so I want to set him right, and you can do it in a moment."

Poor Nick didn't feel much like setting anybody right. He felt horribly ashamed and self-reproachful, as good people generally do when someone else has been doing wrong; but he realised he must somehow shield Lady Atherton in the presence of Colonel Brereton, and he tried to twist his honest, ingenuous Cumberland face into an expression of polite indifference, and came a step or two nearer.

"He says," went on Sir Theodore—"he says Lady Atherton sent you a present, and—"

"She did not," interrupted Nick eagerly, glad to be able to deny something at least. "She did not. I bought it at a bazaar."

"It's immaterial. He says there was a letter!"

"The letter was no concern of his."

"Of course; nor of mine either. I want you to tell him so."

Poor Nick. If he could only have said it! A man more adroit, but equally truthful, could easily have said that at any rate the letter concerned neither himself nor Lady Atherton, since it was neither directed nor signed, and bore no resemblance to Lady Atherton's hand, but Nick wasn't half quick enough to think of that. Besides, of all the letters he had received from her, none bore any resemblance to any of the others. So he only said, "There is some mistake."

"Of course.   That's what I say; but—" he hesitated, turned from Nick to Brereton, who stood angry and grave.   There was no trace of any " I told you so " look on his face—only intense sorrow for his friend.   Atherton considered for a moment, then he said :—

"The best thing will be for you to show us the letter."

Nick started back, instinctively grasping at the place where the letter was.   Whether it was meant for him or another did not matter.   All he knew was that he must not show it.

"I can't do that," he cried; "no, I can't do that."

"It will be much the best," repeated Atherton.

" I can't."

"That is all, Atherton," said Colonel Brereton quietly.   "It is well I spoke; but we had better go now, I suppose," and he laid his hand almost tenderly on his friend's arm.   Atherton shook him off impatiently, turning to Durthwaite.

" Do you see the impression you are giving ? "

" I can't help it," said Nick.   "If you had only come alone—"

" I will go," said Brereton ; " you'll find me at the club, Ted." ·

" Oh, confound it ! " cried Atherton, worried into temper.   " How you're annoying me.   Don't you see it's you I want to have convinced ?   Mr. Durthwaite, kindly show us that letter."

"No," said Nick.

"You refuse definitely to show it?"

"I can't show it."

Atherton gave an angry laugh, and walked to the window and looked out a moment or two, then he turned to the room again. "I don't know which of you is worse," he said fretfully. "Tom, don't you forget Muriel's story. Mr. Durthwaite, it would give me the most intense pleasure to get that letter for myself, since you won't give it; but that sort of thing won't do. So perhaps you will kindly come with us just now. I see the cab we came in is still waiting."

Nick assented. Anything would be better than to expose Lady Atherton.

"Where are we going?" said Brereton, as he followed the others downstairs.

"We are going to Lady Atherton, because she is the only one among us who has a grain of common sense."

Lady Atherton was not alone when the three entered the drawing-room, but her companion vanished through the curtains into the room beyond, as they came forward into the light. Lady Atherton had been crying a little apparently, but she looked wonderfully pretty.

All Sir Theodore's annoyance and perplexity disappeared when he began to speak to his wife, but his fluency went with them.

"Muriel," he began lamely, "it's all nonsense and I am sorry to bother you about it, but *he's* got hold of some mad idea about a sachet you made with a letter in it to *him*," indicating each with a faint movement, "and he wouldn't show it, so we came to you."

Sir Theodore seemed to think he had done his part now, for he dropped into a chair and left things to take their course.

"What is it all about, Mr. Durthwaite? Why should you not show any of my letters?"

At that moment it flashed in Durthwaite's mind what an utter fool he had been not to *know* it was all right.

"I didn't know much of Colonel Brereton, and Sir Theodore wanted me to show it to *him*. There is some mistake." He handed her the letter.

An excited flash rose to her face as she read it. Her eyes gleamed indignantly as she looked at Colonel Brereton. "And you distrusted me?" she said. Then he too suddenly felt ashamed and ridiculous, and had nothing to say.

"Am I to see it?" said Sir Theodore, placidly.

"No, dear; it is for Colonel Brereton to see." She handed him the sheet.

"Teddy," she went on, turning to her husband, "he ought to have had that letter years ago. I told you I should ask Kate Haydon about that story. I have been asking her this afternoon. She is so quiet and reticent, she would have kept silent until the end of the world if I hadn't. It appears she used to be very fond of Colonel Brereton ; but he was very wild then, you know, and had no prospects. You remember what her people were like, so strict and so money-loving. They could have put up with the worst of character if it hadn't been for the want of money ; but they would not hand her over to probable perdition and certain poverty. So they made the worst of his want of repute, and persecuted her awfully ; but all the same she would have been faithful to him if he had only been sure he loved her."

"She wrote this to me years ago," broke in Colonel Brereton, "and I never got it. She loved me all the time while I thought—where is she, Lady Atherton ? Presently I will come and beg for your forgiveness, but now I must see her. Where is she ?" Lady Atherton pointed towards the inner room.

"You will find her there. Go to her and you will be much happier than you deserve."

"Go on, Muriel," said Sir Theodore, as he left them.

"That's almost all. All that time Miss Haydon was making a wedding present for me, and by some strange blunder the letter must have got inside it, and lain there till Grédel took it out in mistake for a packet of autographs. When the poor girl received no answer, she let herself be worried into accepting the other man, who died ; but I don't understand how you came to have the letter, Mr. Durthwaite ? "

"Oh, I ?   Well, you know, I'd seen you make it —the sachet, I mean—and it was so beautiful, and — and—I admire both of you so much, that I just went down to Clayton, and bought it, you know. I do hope you won't mind."

Sir Theodore burst into a hearty good-tempered laugh ! "What enthusiasm !" he cried. "Why, if you wanted it, why on earth didn't you ask for it ? You'd have given it him, wouldn't you, Muriel ? At any rate, since his appreciation of your work has brought about such a satisfactory discovery for us all, the least you can do is to sew him a dozen or two of handkerchiefs to put in it."

THE ADMIRAL'S GOOD NATURE.

The Admiral's Good Nature.

THE "Admiral's" visiting cards only described
him as "Lieut. Lawrence A. Busshe, R.N.,"
but all his friends had agreed to promote him
simply as an expression of goodwill, because he was
the best natured fellow in the world, and because
they were all so fond of him.

He came cantering round the corner beside the
shabby palings that bounded the grounds of Devern
Court just as Gracia Slade, who was staying there
with her aunt, came towards the gate from the
opposite direction. He sprang to the ground and
waited for her, leaning against the gate.

"Good morning, Miss Slade, I am told that we
are all to congratulate you."

"Oh don't," she said, laughing a little, as she gave
him her hand with the pretty, graceful self-consciousness of a very young girl newly engaged. "I have
been receiving congratulations all the morning, and
it is so unpleasant."

"Is it now?" he said, a little surprised. "I should not have thought so; I fancy I should rather like it."

She looked at him for a moment as if she were going to answer him in an ordinary, commonplace way, and then began to laugh instead.

Larry Busshe laughed too, because if there was a joke going he would not be left out in the cold; then he asked her what amused her.

"I could not conceive of you being congratulated on your engagement to a *Miss* Perth—if there was one—and, of course, you can't understand how a girl feels when she is congratulated."

"Well, *Mr.* Perth likes it; I heard him being congratulated yesterday, that was how I knew of the affair. I congratulated him myself, and he seemed to enjoy it."

"Ah, that's natural enough," she said.

Looking into the girl's very sweet young face, and great grey-blue eyes, Larry thought so too, only he was a little surprised that she should say so.

"Of course there is no question which of you has most right to congratulation," he answered.

The girl laughed again.

"Oh, I don't mean that," she said. "It did sound like it, what I said, didn't it? I only mean—well, something like this—a man is at least *supposed* to have made an effort, and won a victory, and we are supposed to have surrendered, given in, as it were, not won a victory at all. I don't think I *ran after* Mr. Perth, did I? I didn't persuade him to marry me? At least I don't think I did anything of the sort, and yet I have been congratulated until I feel as if I had done something very difficult and clever by dint of very hard trying. As if I had come to Devern Court on purpose to marry Mr. Perth, and by 'patient and unremitting attention to business' had attained my object at last. As if I had studied for him like a competitive examination, and now had passed, and got my diploma, and ought to be very proud of myself."

"Well, some of the girls did, you know; you see living down here they had nothing else to do. I think, under the circumstances, it is very kind of them to congratulate you, and you ought to take it in a better spirit."

"I suppose I ought," she said. "Of course every-one likes to be married, for if one is not married one has to be an old maid, and that's hateful. Besides," she added, seriously, " Mr. Perth is such a very good man."

"Oh."

Larry was a careless, light-hearted man, not given to seeing the serious side of life; he did not know or think how tragic a confession such words carry when spoken by a young girl of her lover. When some few days before he had heard that Gracia Slade was engaged to Mr. Alexander Perth, of Market Devern Bank, he had felt that momentary regret that most men feel on hearing that a very pretty girl is engaged to someone else: a regret that is half resentment at the girl's thoughtlessness in not waiting to see if they were not going to propose to her themselves. Larry had experienced this resentful regret lightly and good-naturedly very many times where other pretty girls had been concerned, but Gracia Slade was by far the most beautiful girl he had ever seen. Her features were so delicate, and her skin so fair, that it seemed as if made only of soft lights and shadows, as though if one touched it one's hand would go through and leave no trace, any more than in rose-coloured light, or the reflection of lilies in water. He had seen her once or twice when she was a child, and she had been pretty then, but he had no idea that she would grow into such a woman as this, and so he was inclined to resent her engagement very much indeed.

Larry Busshe had the Irish worship of beauty even more strongly developed than the usual run of his countrymen. His friends never suspected this, because he was always so attentive to plain girls. That was his good nature, he was so terribly sorry for them. He could not conceive of life having any attraction whatever for plain women, so he did his best, when he met the poor creatures, to give them a good time, and help them to forget their great misfortune, on the same principle as he would have modified his brisk swinging stride to the feeble gait of a cripple, rather than remind him of his infirmity by outstripping him.

"Is the wedding to be soon?" he asked.

"My aunt and Mr. Perth want it to be very soon," she said.

He could understand that easily enough; the selfish, commonplace banker was wise there, for if he waited, this charming girl would find out that there were much better fellows than he in the world, and change her mind. Still, it was a shame she should be hurried into a marriage with a man whose goodness she was driven to assert so much more to convince herself than to impress her hearer. He did not quite know what to say. He certainly was not likely to offend her again by congratulating her. She was stroking his horse's great arched neck and soft black nose ; what a picture they made, the two of them ! The sight supplied him with an idea.

"Well, you'll let me congratulate you on Perth's horses, won't you? He bought three such hunters last week as made me wish I had been a banker. For your use, of course ; we shall have you cutting us all out in the hunting field, I suppose, by and by."

"No ; I think not. I—I don't hunt."

"Oh, but you will, of course ; Perth will soon teach you to ride."

"I can ride," she said with dignity. "I used to have a pony and ride a great deal at home, but Mr. Perth does not approve of ladies hunting."

"What, live at Devern and not hunt? Why, no-body ever comes to Devern except for the hunting. How will you pass your time?"

"Why, as I always have done, I suppose," she answered quietly. "I have not been in the habit of hunting."

Larry felt quite indignant. The poor girl didn't know what she was losing. What, to come straight from school to stay in a dull country house, and then be handed over to a dull man, who wanted to make a domestic drudge of her from the very first! Was the girl to have no fun in her life at all? It would have been different if she had not been so pretty ; a plain girl might well marry a "very good man," and be thankful, but this girl had a right to expect life to be pleasant.

"Oh, look here! that won't do," he said. "We can't let him make a married nun of you that way I shall see Perth at Blakeley Common to-morrow, and tell him I knew your father, and I won't stand it."

"He won't be at Blakeley."

"Why, I shouldn't have thought he'd miss Blake-ley ; we always get such easy runs when we meet there."

When he saw what he had implied he was sorry, and afraid that she would be vexed ; but she had not noticed anything amiss in his speech, and went on herself, just a little indignantly,

"He is in Sunderland on business. He won't be back for a day or two. I think he might have offered to send a horse and groom over and let me ride about among the lanes quietly. At least"—recollecting herself—"I mean I am sure he would, if he had known how much I should like it."

"I am sure of it," said Larry promptly. "He only wants educating. See here, Miss Slade, I am an old friend of your father's. I knew you when you were a child. I really feel quite chaperonishly towards you (he was some nine years her elder) ; so, when you come to think of it, it is quite my duty to look after you. Now, suppose you were to take a quiet ride with me, Blakeley way, you know, and we were to see the meet, and keep them in sight as we went along the roads, you know, and, perhaps, if you felt equal to it, go a little farther? Don't you think it would be very pleasant?"

"Oh." Her flushed face and eager child's eyes showed how pleasant she found even the prospect. "Oh, do you think it would be right?"

"Quite right ; just the rightest thing we could do ; I'm sure of it. Why should you not have a little pleasure when you can?"

"I don't quite see how I can manage it," she said, with a regret in her tone that made him all the more eager to do her this little kindness.

"It is very simple, tell your aunt you want to come, and come."

"But she won't let me. She is very strict. She always is telling me that I am inclined to be 'giddy,' and if I don't take care she will send me away, and

T

adopt my sister instead.   And besides, I can't ask her.   She went away to stay a few days with friends this morning.   Dear old Frances and I are to go to Saint Leonards to-morrow morning, and take rooms, and wait there for aunt till her visit is over."

"Then it is still simpler.   Put on your habit in the morning, start for Saint Leonards ; get out at Blakeley Station—the trains all stop there—and I will meet you there with the horses.   Frances can either take your luggage on, and meet you in the evening, or wait for you at Blakeley."

"Oh I should like it so much," she said.

"You would once you got started.   There is no pleasure in life like a good run."

"Ah," she cried, laughing, "then you mean a run, after all ? "

"Well, yes, if I find you equal to it ; will you come ? "

She ought to have known better, but she said yes. She was so young, and had such a healthy youthful longing for fun, and so very little opportunity of indulging in it ; and he ought to have known better, and considered that he might get the girl into a quarrel with her relative and with her *fiancé*, but he didn't.   Probable consequences never troubled him very much.   He only thought that he was going to give a very nice girl a good time ; if he did reflect that he was to‧ have a very good time himself into the bargain, why it was only fair that his good nature, his one virtue, should be rewarded.

He was early at Blakeley Station next morning, and Unkas, his big iron-grey horse, plunged and flung all over the place when the train came in, while Paquita, the gentle, well-trained bay mare he had brought for Gracia, stood steady and indifferent, only looking at Unkas with eyes of gentle contempt, as if to ask, "Why waste your energy in this folly, since we shall have plenty to excite us by-and-bye?"

"Is SHE what you've brought for me?   Oh, what a darling!" cried Gracia, looking right into Paquita's gentle eyes, and knowing that she would be perfectly happy in her company.   "Oh! you lucky man to have such a creature for your own!   Frances is with me.   She is going to wait here, and we will go on together in the evening.   She's got a book, and her knitting, and some lunch, but I am afraid she will be awfully dull; only she said she should be anxious about me if I wouldn't let her stay.   She is such a dear woman."

Frances was standing by, looking, half in distress, half in admiration, at her pretty mistress.   She was a fresh-looking, elderly woman, with a pleasant, ugly face.   As she bent forward to brush a little dust off Gracia's shoulder, Larry told himself that she was a good, appreciative, trustworthy creature, and wondered if he could find an excuse for giving her five shillings.

"I'll take care of her, Frances," he called, as they rode off.

Frances said, "I hope so, sir," and Gracia looked round and nodded to her; and then they both forgot everything but the pleasure of their expedition together.

"Oh, she is a darling—a darling!" cried Gracia, stroking Paquita's satiny neck, and bending forward as if she would like to kiss it. "Why, I feel as if I had known her all my life—or ought to have done. I feel as if I had lived in her saddle. 'Admiral'— oh, I beg your pardon, but father always used to call you 'Admiral'—Mr. Busshe, I mean; last time you saw me you gave me some sweets—such a lot. I remember I treated all the girls when I went back to school, and enjoyed them tremendously, but not as I am enjoying myself to-day. Don't you think it is a privilege to be able to give your fellow-creatures so much pleasure?"

"Oh, yes, that's just it. I do it from benevolence," he said, laughing.

"There isn't any enjoyment like it in the world," she cried—"like riding, I mean. This lovely lane, the glorious motion, the air in one's face, the feeling of power over this noble creature. Shall you mind if I love Paquita as much as you do? It is not only that she is beautiful, Mr. Busshe, but I feel that she is *good*. She has fire and courage enough for anything; but she wouldn't do anything she shouldn't, simply because she is good. I feel immense confidence in her already."

"And you're right," he cried, his warmest feelings

roused when his favourite mare was praised. "If I hadn't known her by heart I wouldn't have put you on her, you may be sure. She is as safe as a church and as gentle as a lamb, for all her spirit. See, now, here are three roads; go as if you meant taking the left, and then change your mind, and with half a tremour of your wrist turn her sharp off to the right. There, isn't that a mouth for you? See how she answers the helm—quick and quiet, like a perfect wife."

"Oh, don't say that," she laughed; "that's like one of Mr. Perth's ideas."

Again neither noticed the hint of tragedy in the idle words—that this girl was going to marry a man for whom she cared so little that she wanted to forget all about him in her moments of enjoyment, and was so young and foolish and light-hearted that she did not see what such a marriage meant. Had she been older and wiser, and knowing what she was doing, had done it deliberately, there would have been less ground for pity; but had she been older or wiser she would not have done it at all. That was where the tragedy came in. She probably thought she was doing very well for herself.

So they rode on together, he only thinking that the clear sweep of the line of her cheek from the ear to the chin, the graceful curve downwards of the flaxen eyebrow, the delicate profile against the sky, were all graces miles beyond such a savage as Perth's deserving, and that it was a thousand pities such a ride as this should be a solitary pleasure for them both, and not the first of many.

"Where is the meet?" she asked.

"Oh, we are late for the meet! They must have found by now; and I take it, judging from my very limited knowledge and experience of these parts, that we shall come on them in a few moments."

"Mr. Busshe, did you miss the meet because of me?"

"Yes, I did. Philanthropy again, as I said—pure philanthropy."

"But I could have taken an earlier train."

"Well, I thought missing the meet would be a good excuse for keeping to the roads if you did not feel like going across country."

"But I do—I do," she cried. "I'll go anywhere with Paquita. I couldn't be afraid on her."

"You know what you can do better than I. I'll be quite content to keep to the roads."

"But I shall not. I am all right. Don't be anxious about me. Didn't I tell you I was used to riding? Oh, Admiral, look! There they are— there they are!"

Yes, there they were, the whole field, coming down at right angles to them, about three fields away. He and she could strike across, and be up with the best of them in next to no time, if they choose.

He hesitated half a moment, looking at her as she sat, straight and easy and confident, but wild with excitement.

" All right," he said. " But steady, steady; don't rush at big fences too early in the day. There is a gate a little further along. Come on."

There was a gate, and on the other side of it a wide stretch of pasture land, then a low earth bank, and another meadow, then a shallow brook that they splashed through, then a ploughed field, where Gracia felt herself a little shaken, then a paling that those in front had considerably broken down, so that Unkas and Paquita took it in their stride; after that a great stretch of moorland with gorse growing on it, and little shallow pools lying here and there, and birds fluttering up startled from before their horses' feet, and over all the sweet, fresh, scented air.

" Oh, it's lovely, lovely!" she cried. " It's just like what I have read about, only is it always as easy as this ? "

He laughed.

" Oh, dear, no ; this is mere drawing-room work, so to speak, not hunting. There aren't any real fences in these parts. It's as safe as the ' Row,' only more fun."

" Why, aren't there any five-barred gates, or ten-foot hedges, or twenty-foot brooks, or churches, or monuments ? I feel like getting over anything."

" Ah ! he's heading Catesby way ; you'll have a fence or two before long."

They were riding side by side, well up with the hunt, but a little to the left of the crowd, because he could best take proper care of her so, and because it was so very pleasant to have this sweet girl all to himself, out of the crowd, riding side by side with him, turning every now and then such glowing, deep grey eyes on him as they rode, as if to insist on his sharing alll the keen enjoyment she felt.

The sharp turn to the right towards Catesby had, of course, left Busshe and Gracia some way behind ; so they quickened their pace a little. A narrow ditch separated the moor from a meadow where some sleepy old cows blundered out of the way as the dogs and horses swept through. Busshe and Gracia almost caught up with the rest before they had left the meadow. There was a low hedge at the end of it, separating it from a lane. Everyone got over safely and clattered down the lane.

"Don't hurry, Gracia," Busshe called. "There's sure to be a gate."

She laughed. "I wouldn't hurt Paquita's feelings by taking her through any more gates," she cried, and rode straight at the hedge.

Well, why not ? She looked fit enough. Paquita rose at the hedge firmly and gracefully, like the curl of a great wave on a still day, and the girl's face flashed past him like the spirit of delight.

And then, while it just occurred to him, as the mare rose, that Gracia did not know that she had been bred in Ireland, and ought to have been warned to sit fast when the mare changed feet, somehow it was all over; Paquita had landed as easily as the wave when it curls over and breaks on the soft sand, but Gracia was lying stretched straight out on the ground, with her face against the stones.

Even then he was not much alarmed, it was not much of a fall, and he had seen a good many. He called out "Are you hurt?" and was at her side in a moment. Then raising her, to lay her along the soft bank till she should get her breath, he saw what had happened.

Her face had been dashed against the sharp stones. One glance at it was enough, too much. It was as if a pink blossom had lain under a waggon wheel.

And he had done this! He had done it in his light-hearted egotism : just for a day's pleasure— at a whim's dictation, he had done this.

The girl moaned feebly, unconscious, but feeling the pain through her unconsciousness.

He turned away his eyes for a moment's rest from the sight of the poor mutilated face, and there was Paquita, standing still as a sentinel, looking at him with great astonished reproachful eyes, as if to say,

"Why did you do it? Why did you put the girl on me, and let me take the fence, if she couldn't ride? It is not my fault, but yours."

This was more than he could bear, and he burst out crying like a child.

Why had he done it, indeed? Why had he not known, that her light-hearted confidence was but the confidence of ignorance? "I used to ride a great deal on my pony." Why, the merest fool should have known what that had meant.

He took her up in his arms, covering her face with his handkerchief. The farm where he had taken up his quarters for the season was not very far distant, and he knew of no other place in the neighbourhood where he could take her, so he decided to carry her there, and send for a doctor.

He forgot all about the horses; he just left them in the lane, and went on carrying the girl's passive weight in his arms, scarcely conscious of the fatigue of it in his horror and remorse.

He had meant, for her beauty's sake, to give her one day's pleasure, and it had cost her all the beauty and pleasure of all her life. For what joy could life or youth give to the poor child now? All her young life was laid waste, and his recklessness had done it.

He stopped at a brook to bathe the girl's face, but she moaned so when he touched it that he gave up the attempt, thinking it would be better to wait for a doctor, so he replaced the handkerchief, and set out again.

Then he saw Joseph Perth coming across a field towards him, and realised another cause for self-reproach. This woman, whom he had so injured, belonged to another man. It was another man's wife whom he had changed from such beauty to such horror. He had wronged the man almost as much as the woman.

He stood still for Perth to come up.

"What does this mean, Mr. Busshe?" Perth said angrily. "I returned sooner than I expected, and am told Miss Slade has been hunting to-day in your company. I hope I am misinformed."

"You see," said Larry, tersely.

"Then do you think it was proper conduct to persuade an affianced young lady to act directly contrary to the expressed wishes of her future husband?"

Perth shouted the words insolently and loudly over the hedge, while he looked for an easy place to climb. Larry did not resent the tone. What right had he to resent anything this girl's lover might say? If Perth were to turn on him and strike him with his riding-whip he should not resent it; it would be a relief to him.

"The poor girl didn't know the danger," he said slowly. "I made her come; you're right, it is all my fault, the poor girl isn't to blame."

"That is a point I will discuss with her," said Perth, who had got over the hedge now. "I do not require anyone to interfere between my wife that is to be and myself. I am speaking of your conduct. I can say what I like about that, I suppose?"

Yes, indeed, he might say what he liked, because no mere injurious words could equal the injury done to him. And he did not even know of it. Poor heart-broken Larry must tell him.

"It will be a lesson to Miss Slade whom to trust in future."

"Perth," said Larry, still half sobbing, "don't you see she is hurt?"

"No," said Perth, surprised; "they told me it was nothing, that she was up again in a minute."

"They were mistaken."

"Good God, she's not dead?" Perth cried, He had been too much engrossed by his own anger and wounded dignity to give much thought to Gracia before, but now he was both frightened and horrified, and stared at Busshe breathlessly.

"No, not dead, nor any bones broken, but you see she has fainted."

"Give her to me, please. I wonder the idea did not occur to you sooner. She will be better in my care than yours, and will feel safer seeing me than you when she comes to, I should say, considering the care you have taken of her so far. Where are you going?"

Busshe told him.

Perth grunted. "It would have been better to have kept by the horses till she came to, and let her mount again. Is it far to the farm? I fancy we had better wait and rest a little."

He thought there was nothing worse than a mere fainting fit, and Larry tried to summon courage to tell him the truth.

"If you had had any sense you would have asked someone for some brandy," grumbled Perth. "She would have come round in a minute then."

"I have brandy."

"Then why on earth didn't you give her some? You had better give her some now."

Mechanically Larry took out his flask and raised the handkerchief.

Perth gave a positive scream of horror as he saw.

"Good God! Busshe, take her," he cried. "I can't hold her, I can't look at her. Take her, I say, or she'll fall."

Busshe took her, and Perth reeled up against a tree, shuddering, and as white as a sheet.

"Give me some of that brandy," he said. "I shall faint or be sick; I never saw such a sight. My God! I'd rather you had killed her than done that. And I was to have had the loveliest wife in England."

"The sooner we get a doctor to her the better," Busshe said, holding Gracia very tenderly. "Take some brandy, and then perhaps you will be able to think of her a little more and yourself a little less."

"Where does the nearest doctor live?" Perth asked eagerly. "I'll go and send him. You must take her on to the farm, I can't. It's not so bad for you; you were not to have married her."

"But you'll come back with him? She'll want to see you. Remember what you said yourself; she'd rather see you than me when she comes to. Try to command yourself for her sake."

"I can't; I can't bear to look at her. You must stay with her. You did it, and you must see her through it. I'll send the nearest doctor."

Yes, that was true.   He did it, and he must see her through it.   So, while Perth hurried away across the fields scared and trembling, he covered the girl's face again, and carried her tenderly and carefully to the farm.

He sent off a messenger at once for Frances, and when the doctor came sat beside Gracia, holding her hands all the dreadful time while her injured face was being dressed.

She was conscious then—conscious, at least, of the pain, and of his presence, and the strength it gave her, for though he felt her hands in his vibrate and quiver with agony, she would not cry out ; and when it was all over she was able to thank him faintly, but still sweetly, for staying with her, and " not minding."

There was not any danger—at least, no danger to life, or limb, nor even, as the doctor had half-feared at first, to her brain.   She would recover ; with care she would recover soon ; but—well, when Larry thought of what that lovely girl would look like when she came out of the darkened room, he half forgave Perth for his selfish cry, " I had rather you had killed her."

She was quite ignorant, too, of the extent of the misfortune which had befallen her, for though the doctor had no fear for her brain, still it was best to avoid any shock to her feelings as yet.   She believed readily enough that the darkened room meant only care for her eyesight.

Larry left the farm, of course, and gave up his quarters there to Gracia and her maid ; but he saw her daily for a few moments, and each time her hopefulness of a quick recovery went near to break his heart.

He learned from Frances that Perth had not been once to see her.

Presently the day grew near for Larry to join his ship. In the excitement of all this trouble he had forgotten how near the time was. He had to go to town for a few days to arrange his business affairs, and on his return to Blakeley went to see Gracia again.

She was a great deal better, so the farm people told him, yet it struck him they looked more sorry for her than ever. Frances came upstairs with him, and he was sure she had been crying.

He found the shutters in the bedroom partly opened. Gracia was allowed a little light now, she told him.

There was only a little light in the room, but enough. Well the change was no greater than he had expected from the first, and she was still unconscious of it, or believed that it would be only temporary ; he sat down beside her, and began to speak as cheerfully as he could.

"Oh, I am going to talk a great deal to-day," she said, "I am so much better now. I am quite well enough to get up and go about, only I can't with all this sticking-plaster on my face. I hope if I have any scars they won't be big ones; but that run we had was worth a scratch or two, wasn't it?"   .

She looked up laughing, at Frances apparently; but no, Frances had left the room, she was waiting for him to answer, but her eyes—her beautiful eyes —seemed to be staring quite another way. What did this mean?

He guessed only too soon, though he did not learn the reason till later, strabismus had developed, and this was the result. The poor girl squinted so frightfully, that even with no other disfigurement she would be hideous.

Hurriedly catching at the first idea that came to him lest she should notice his dismay, he asked her if her aunt was not coming to her.

She laughed. "My aunt has disowned me. I expected it. She is going to adopt my sister. Frances and I are left to our own devices."

" Has Perth forgiven me yet?"

" Mr. Perth? Oh I don't think you need trouble about him.   He sent once to enquire after me, and sent me some fruit. I believe Frances gave it to the school children, she did not bring it upstairs. Groundless jealousy is very contemptible."

Her quiet cold tone spoke more than her words.

Busshe understood. She thought Perth's desertion was the result of jealousy, not knowing of any other cause. A short while ago he had lightly pitied this lovely girl for throwing herself away on a man not good enough for her, and to think that he should come to pity her as a poor disfigured wreck, whose one chance of making a good settlement he had destroyed.

For it came to that, and the harsh, coarse idea carried so much meaning. The great gulf between beauty and ugliness was passed. A beautiful young girl, a prosperous wife, finds life made so pleasant for her; but who would make the rough places smooth, or the hard ways soft for Gracia now? All her life now, from its young beginning to old age, would be hard and lonely and loveless through him. The thought came to him that it was his duty to save her from such a fate.

"I am not sorry."

She was speaking to him, and he started, but did not answer. She went on :—

"I would rather live alone all my life than marry a man I did not really love."

"And did you not?"

"No, I thought I did; I liked having a lover. I suppose all girls fresh from school like that. It seems so grand and grown up. I thought I was content—pleased, even; but I know better now."

"What taught you, dear?"

She did not speak, but her hand on the coverlet moved an inch towards him.

His vast pity and the enthusiasm of his resolve lent a force and strength to his next words that might even have satisfied a woman who knew what love was.

U

"Was it I, dear? Was it that you found you could love me better? Will you? Will you if I tell you how very much I want you to marry me?"

"Yes, Admiral, I think it was that, and I think I will."

Remember that she did not know she was not the beautiful girl she had been; remember she had noted with a schoolgirl's quickness, and set a schoolgirl's exaggerated value on his open admiration, and don't blame her for yielding so easily.

Then he told her how he must leave to join his ship the next evening, and would go up to town that night and get a license so that they could be married in the morning. She did not like the idea at all.

"Oh, we had much better wait till you come back, Admiral. You won't be long away, and I shall be well by the time you are here again. It would be horrid to be married in a dressing-gown, without any orange-blossoms, or cake, or *trousseau.* Why, I shouldn't even be able to see you while I was saying 'I will,' for they won't let me look at anything—not even at a glass to see if Frances has done my hair right. I don't wonder, for there is something hurting me dreadfully, close to one of my eyes; but the doctor says it will be better soon. Don't you really think we had better wait till you come home? I shan't change my mind again this time. I am very sure of it now," she added, softly.

" My dear," he said, bending closer, " you do not know what a comfort it will be to me to go away feeling that we are safely married."

It was true enough, for he was afraid that if he did not act in the first flush of his generous impulse that he should lose courage, or perhaps that she would find out the truth, and refuse to allow the sacrifice to be made. Since the thing was right to do, the sooner it was done the better.

So, after talking a little longer, she gave in, and agreed to his plan, and submitted to his leaving her then, as he had not much time left if he was to catch the evening train.

" Good-bye," she said, holding up her face to be kissed as a matter of course (she had been engaged before). " Don't kiss the sticking-plaister—take the other side."

He laid the golden head on his breast, and kissed the poor face where he could ; and when the loving blue-grey eyes that were looking at him seemed to be bestowing their tenderness at random over the room, he told himself that the tragedy only needed that element of the ridiculous in it to be complete.

He left her. Frances met him at the foot of the stairs. She was crying.

" Oh, sir—sir," she sobbed, " have you seen her ? One wouldn't so much have minded a scar or two, but this—this! And you promised to take care of her."

" Yes, Frances, and I broke my word, but I will

keep it in the future. We are going to be married."

Old Frances stared at him a moment, and then forgetting her place, and the stately dignity becoming the well-trained old family servant that she was, she threw her arms round his neck and kissed him.

.   .   .   .   .   .

Larry Busshe was coming home sooner than he had expected ; he had written to Gracia telling her when he should arrive at the little house at Maidenhead, which he had found time to take before leaving, ready for his wife to go to, when she should be well enough for the removal. Just now he was reading over her last letter to him.

" Dear Admiral," it began,

" This letter will be more legible than the others, because they are beginning to let me have a little more light, but I have had that horrid pain close to my eyes again, so I have not got well quite so soon as I hoped to do. Frances has been reading to me, I don't know what the book was about, because the first sentence set me thinking about you, it was—

" ' Before marriage a man revels in the thought of how he loves his mistress, afterwards he prefers to think how much she loves him.'

" If that is true I may tell you how I love you now, may I not? I don't think I did in the other letters—at least, not enough—but I don't think I can ever tell you *quite* enough. Did you know I admired you dreadfully when I was a child? And then father was always praising you and saying what a good fellow you were. (He didn't know quite what a good fellow you are, but I do, don't I?) And I used to be so proud of talking about you to the girls at school. Greedy things, they only thought of the sweets, but I thought about you, though I liked the sweets too, mind (you always used to send such nice ones). I laugh now to think of myself sitting in the swing, after lessons, sucking caramels and thinking how handsome you were. I think about that now, too ; it is very good to be beautiful I think, when people love us, isn't it? We will have a lot of caramels when you come home, and sit and tell each other how nice we are by the hour together, won't we ?

"Oh, I know that life won't be all caramels, even while I am writing such nonsense. I don't forget how you held my hand all the while the doctor was hurting me so, and how your touch made me feel so strong and brave, I didn't even want to cry out and make a fuss, and so hurt you too. Larry, I am going to be such a good wife to you. I am so glad we had that ride together. I love you so much, dear."

The child gave him her love so light-heartedly because she thought it a good gift ; and it had been ! A little while ago her love would have been a good gift for any man to receive ; and now, because the giver was changed, was the gift of no value? She could love just every bit as well as before her sweet face fell among the stones. Was her love to be counted as nothing because of her lost beauty? Would any other man have shrunk as he shrank from the thought of those scars, those eyes? He hardly knew which feeling was stronger in his heart—pity for Gracia, or of himself for having been obliged to marry Gracia as she was.

When he neared the little house in Maidenhead he did not quite know if he were glad or sorry that a wife awaited him in it. As he walked briskly up the little garden path, his mind was so full of Gracia as she used to be, that he grew almost breathless with eagerness, and was half indignant that the door was so long in being opened. He would have liked Gracia to have been on the step waiting for him. When a servant admitted him at last he asked impatiently where his mistress was.

The girl was surprised. She knew nothing of any mistress ; she belonged to the house, and was let with the furniture, and had only kept everything in readiness till the gentleman who had taken the house should come. She had heard nothing from nobody ; only as a letter had come for the gentleman that morning, she had supposed he was coming himself before long.

"Bring me the letter."

It was in Gracia's hand, and had been posted to him before he had written to tell her that he was about to return. He had just missed it when his ship had left, and by some accident of quick forwarding it had reached England before him. He opened it and read.

"I have just seen myself. You shall never see me again.—GRACIA."

Well, was he glad or sorry? Was this liberty or loss? He did not know. He went into the empty house and found it damp and cheerless. The servant brought him in a bad dinner, and he dined very miserably. He saw all his latest letters to Gracia lying unopened on the mantelpiece. "We thought something was wrong," the servant said, "when all those came and no one was here to read them." Yes, something was very wrong indeed.

He sat long in the dark thinking; he could think best of Gracia in the dark. Then he called for lights, and read over that last letter he had received while abroad. How pathetic its lighthearted contents seemed now! Then he read over the letter of farewell, and its despair went straight from her heart to his. Poor pretty Gracia, poor loving, happy-hearted child, he would have given twenty years of his life to have undone that morning's work at Blakeley.

And now she knew the truth, knew the extent of her misfortune, of his fault, and had refused his atonement: he sat thinking of her as she had been, and as she was, and wondering if he were glad or sorry that she had refused it.

It was months before he knew. He went up to town and tried to content himself with his old friends and his old pleasures, but he could not forget Gracia. He told himself it was no wonder that a man could not forget a girl whom he had injured so deeply, and he began to make inquiries for her.

She had left Blakeley Farm, and the people there either did not or would not tell him where she was gone. He wrote to Gracia's aunt, and received a very ill-tempered letter in reply, saying that she had only one niece now, Miss Violet Slade, and knew nothing whatever of Mrs. Busshe's movements. Then he wrote to Mr. Perth, and had his letter returned marked " gone abroad."

It seemed that the poor child was deserted by all her other friends. Clearly then it became his duty to find and care for his wife, whether she would or not, so he began to search for her in real earnest.

The search was more difficult and tedious than he had imagined it would be, and after a few weeks spent in fruitless inquiries it occurred to him to advertise in the newspapers.

He worded his advertisement, " Gracia is entreated to write to L.B.," but no answer came to the address he had given ; at least no answer from Gracia, but after the advertisement had appeared once or twice it seemed to have attracted notice, for he received endless letters from idle folks commiserating him on Gracia's obduracy. He received, too, some execrable verses, with the refrain, "But why don't she write to L.B.?" He even got letters from more than one good-natured young lady offering herself in consolation, but never a word from Gracia. He changed the advertisement at last to, "If Gracia knew how I want her, she would come," but he hoped nothing from it.

At last, thinking the dreariness of the empty house at Maidenhead would be better than the tedium of his life in town, he went home, and tried to make himself feel more cheerful by imagining how the dreary little place would change when Gracia came to it.

He sat beside the fire reading those two last letters again. What a change, what a terrible change from the sweet light-hearted love of one to the heart-broken cry of despair in the other. And somehow it came about, as he read them, that he knew that it was for his own sake, not hers, that he wanted Gracia back ; not for duty, but for love.

He tried to remember his letters to her. Had they been such that reading them in the light of her new knowledge of her disfigurement she had been able to see that he had only married her because he pitied her? Would she never know how he loved her now ?

For he did love her ; love is such a strange erratic deity, there is no accounting for the freaks he will take, but it was certain that Larry Busshe, the fastidious worshipper of beauty, had somehow come to love this poor, scarred, squinting, disfigured woman as truly and as ardently as the most beautiful woman in the world could desire to be loved.

He loved the memory of her beauty, for the sweet voice and sweet words, the loving letter she had written before she knew of her loss of beauty, for the agony of her farewell when she did know of it.

If she would come back! If she would but come! They would sit in the dark together, here, where the fire had sunk low, and he would hold her dear scarred face to his breast, and make her listen while he told her of his love.

If she would come now, while it was dark ; he could think of her best in the dark. If she would only come !

And suddenly, almost as if brought by the force of his longing, Gracia came.

He did not know her step, because all this while he had been learning to love her he had not heard it. The servant announced, " A lady to see you, sir," and left the room, wondering, as usual, at her master's strange fancy for sitting in the dark.

" Do you really want me ? " she said.

" Gracia !   Is it Gracia ? " he cried, and taking her in his arms began to tell her how very much he did want her, kissing her again and again with a fervour no woman could possibly have mistaken for pity.

She laughed—a very happy laugh, and bade him send for lights.

He ordered the lamps immediately, that she might know that he did not shrink from looking upon her. She held her hands over his eyes when the lamps were brought until the servant had left the room.

"Now look at me."

He raised his eyes, bravely and steadily, prepared to see what he might, without a tremor, or the shadow of a sign of shrinking.

What was this? Eyes that met his full and straight and perfect as they were loving; features restored to form and beauty; not a scar, not a fleck. The fair skin just a trifle less soft and transparent perhaps, but, except for that, all the beauty he had seen before that fall in the lane.

He pushed her away with an actual cry of disappointment; now the light had come it seemed he had lost her again.

"What is this?" he cried. "I thought it was Gracia. You are trying to cheat me. You mean well, but I will not be deceived. Who are you? Her sister? I remember she spoke of a beautiful sister, but I don't want her beautiful sister, I want my wife, my poor, brave, marred wife, the wife I love. I want Gracia and no one else."

"Admiral."

There could be no mistaking the voice and tone then; he held out his hands to her in bewilderment.

"Gracia—it is Gracia, it must be, and yet, what does it mean?"

"It means that I am quite well again now, and I love you so much, Admiral."

But it meant more than that, it meant that a very difficult operation had been performed successfully. The doctor who told me this story described what was done; how the eyes were restored to their correct position by cutting the muscles that controlled their actions, and that the scars in the face were easily remedied, though by a process so painful even to hear, that Gracia, who had borne all the suffering bravely, in the hope, after the first passion of despair was over, that the husband who had loved her beauty might, by means of it, some day come to love her, never could bring herself to tell him what she had suffered.

She had seen all his advertisements while she was in the hospital, but divining the spirit of duty that had prompted them, had determined that her husband should not see her till her cure was complete. By the time the cure was complete, the advertisement and the feeling that inspired it were changed.

"Well," as Gracia had said in her letter, "it's good to be beautiful when people love you," and these two found it so, but they found it even better to remember that he had come to love her first when he thought her beauty was gone for ever.

AN UGLY LITTLE WOMAN.

An Ugly Little Woman.

FELIX TENBY stood aside at the crowded barrier to give place to a little nervous flurried woman, who between fear of losing her train, dismay at finding herself unexpectedly in the midst of a noisy crowd, and gratitude to the courteous stranger, became more flurried than ever, got into a muddle with her change, struggled in vain to pick up the slippery ticket with cold, indifferently gloved fingers, and dropped a shower of coppers on the ground.

"Serve you right, Don-Quixote-out-of-date," said the friend who was seeing Tenby off. "You have lost your train through your misplaced gallantry."

The ticket clerk was passing Felix a ticket under another man's arm. He had turned aside from looking after the little flurried woman and laughed.

"Thirty," he said, "and plain at that. Misplaced indeed! The women for whom we do these things owe it to us to be pretty."

She heard, and looked at him. He had not

dreamt of that; he had thought she was gone, but she had just risen from picking up the last copper from under the feet of a hurrying commercial traveller, and had heard the laugh and the words. She looked at him just for a second, not angrily or scornfully as such words deserved, but humbly, deprecatingly, remorsefully almost, as if begging forgiveness for her crime of ugliness. Then she turned her little worn brown face away, and hurried on to the platform. Felix felt as if he had struck a child.

His friend hurried him on to the platform. He did not miss the train after all; it had been delayed a little in consequence of the unusual and unexpected rush of passengers. He had even time to get a paper or two and choose a comfortable carriage, which he had all to himself, for the extra passengers were mostly third class, time to say a few more words to his friend, and laugh over a message or two.

When the train had started, and he was trying to read, the worn, patient little face came back to him, and reproached him. Had there been tears in the eyes? Had he made this poor little creature cry by his vulgar brutality? After all, his words had meant careless irritation that he had, as he thought, missed his train, more than anything else. What right had he to criticise? He was thirty himself— over thirty, and nothing to boast of in the way of beauty; but, then, he was a man.

Surely it must be bad enough to be a woman without having to be an ugly one. Why had God made ugly women? It would have been just as easy to have made them all beautiful.

What makes the joy of manhood? Strength, the knowledge of what is sweet, the power to win and hold it. And of womanhood? Well, women are never quite happy, but they have their joys too. Love, that makes the man's strength theirs—Love, that makes their weakness their pride because it serves as occasion of a lover's tenderness, the sweetness of being a thing desired—the hope of motherhood. But ugly women, what have they of all this? Good God, to be an ugly woman!

How had he come to forget, for he had known this all along; those sad patient eyes reminded him of so much.

To be an ugly woman—to feel with earliest feeling that one is a blot on a beautiful world—to understand, as soon as understanding unfolds, that one's part in life must be to watch while others enjoy, long while others attain, thirst while others drink.

To be an ugly woman—to be an ugly woman and know it.

And thirty years old too, thirty at least—no youth, and no beauty! An ugly woman!

Not always old, though. Once there had been an ugly child—those heart-broken eyes reminded him of it. An ugly child, pushed out of the way perpetually for her beautiful sisters—a failure, an embarrassment to her family, a superfluity. How bitter it all was!

An ugly girl! he remembered it so well, the hopelessness of it, the flat dulness. Not a clever girl either—not one who could have taken ambition by the hand instead of love, or made the beauty of art her beauty. Just a girl, with a girl's wondering curiosity of life, a girl's strange amaze at the growth of first emotions, and possibilities of emotions, a girl's love of love, a girl's sweet, impossible dreams. Soon with a girl's strange new knowledge that one face was more to her than other faces, one voice quicker to reach her ear than all other voices, that one touch had magic in it. He remembered it all.

Yes, that morning, too, when instead of the ordinary dawn of day there was a new creation. The heavens and the earth were made anew, and one little thin brown girl sitting up wondering in her white bed, with a letter clasped fast in her hand, saw that they were very good.

Very good, oh very good! Life was beautiful, the earth glorious, the heavens very near. The letter had done it all.

It was a wonderful letter, for it said she was loved. It spoke tenderly, passionately, strongly. It told how duty called the writer suddenly away, he must leave without seeing her again, but could not leave without telling her his love. He would not be away long, a year at the most; when he came back he should claim her. And would she not write to him meanwhile? Would she not wait for him? Hold herself his, and welcome him when he returned?

Ah, would she not indeed!

And the letter spoke of her beauty! That was puzzling. The little brown girl dropped back on the pillow and rubbed her eyes with her thin hard hand wondering, and read the words again and again many times, then smiled, and kissed the letter, and held it to her bare breast. He remembered it all.

He remembered that studio in the afternoon, the pictures there—and all the while the sweet secret of that letter kept sacredly—looking at the pictures, talking of them, careless words from careless friends, "How bright you are to-day." Ah, it was small wonder, after that letter!

There was a portrait of the artist's wife among the pictures; it was the most beautiful of them all. The artist's wife stood beside it, a vapid commonplace, empty-headed woman, not beautiful at all. The little brown girl looked from her to the portrait, like but glorified, and smiled. "That is how we look to the men who love us," and she pressed her hand on her bodice where the letter rested on her heart; he remembered the sharp pleasure as the rough edge of the envelope pressed against the soft flesh.

After that there had been more letters, all

wonderful, all sweet, and loving, and hopeful. A year of delight, of love, of beauty; for the lover creates beauty by praising it. Oh that year, that pleasant year, how well he remembered it! And the day of triumph, the day when the lover, the creator, was to return: the neat little room, the open window, the scent of fresh turned earth from the ploughed field across the road, the laughter of the birds in the eaves, the laughter of the leaves as they rustled together! He remembered it all—the trembling lips—the breathless eagerness—the burning face, the steps on the gravel, the ring at the bell, the opening door, the suffocating joy.

"My God! it was your sister I meant."

.   .   .   .

Oh it was terrible, terrible, not to be borne; and yet it must be borne; that was the sting of it. The tears rained down his face. Remember? Could such a thing ever be forgotten? The new created earth fell in atoms, the new heavens vanished far out of reach; nothing was left but a little ugly woman, smiling with white lips lest the world should make a mock of her, that such as she had dared to dream of love!

And the days that followed, the long days that followed, they were so burnt into his memory that he doubted if he could forget, even in the ages of eternity; the hourly pain, and the shame of it all.

The agony of watching the happy love of sister and lover—the fuss of preparation for the wedding—to sit and sew at wedding clothes that shrouded her own love—to see her lover pouring out his love upon that careless bright girl, who had many lovers, who had not thought of him till now—to hear his friendly praise of herself—as " such a sensible girl," take his careless greeting and go from the room that the happy lovers might be left together.

And the thoughtless wounding of curious friends. " Well, my dear, I must say I think you behaved very well about it. And so you gave him up? All a mistake, you say; dear! dear! what a pity! And you don't mind? Now that's so brave of you."

So brave? yes, but to the weak courage is anguish.

Oh the longing to end it all—to cry out, " Give me one kiss, and then let me die."

But pride forbade death, for to die was to confess her unsought love to the world. There was no choice but to endure, endure, endure—always endure.

And the dreariness of it, after the sharp agony of parting, the long pain of loneliness, the days without comfort, the years without hope, the daily death of youth ; youth that should die in child-bed, bringing forth to time accomplished hopes, but her youth died sterile.

And the long dull days of life at home, the drudgery of duty uncrowned by love, the thankless service to parents who cared so much less for her unselfish devotion than for the beauty and success of their more fortunate child, and even when they died, were more moved by the brief shallow sorrow of the happy wife than by the long patient watchfulness of the ugly daughter.

And the bitterness of dependence in the house of that fortunate sister, the careless, tolerant pity of the man she had loved—to feel her love die in contempt, and be more desolate for the loss of it—to look on the great sorrow of her life as a thing of shame, of scorn, food for mirth rather than tears; cruel mirth, the tears were less bitter.

The shame of living where she was not wanted, a superfluity in a full life, a discredit, with her plain face and dowdy figure, in a pleasant home!

And the futile efforts to earn her own living, the bitterness of seeing the way made so easy for the young and bright and hopeful, but so hard for her; of seeing the stronger push past her, the fairer chosen before her. The tragic pain of the past was almost sweet, compared with the squalid misery of the present.

There is something in great agony that in itself strengthens us to endurance, but who can endure contempt? In the past she had been wounded and crushed, now every touch was agony, and no one spared her, why should they? What graces had she that should win tenderness, a little faded ugly woman, a mark for the mirth of the young and thoughtless, the dislike of the sensuous, the impatience of the strong? Nothing left her but patience, and she had grown so very weary of patience. Life would have been easier if she could have been angry, but she had no cause for anger. The world loves beauty, and youth, and happiness, and she was old, and sad, and ugly.

The world was full of love, but not for her. The world lives on hope, and she was hopeless; the world is very beautiful, and she was a stain upon it.

"Oh God! to be a woman, and old, and ugly."

It broke his heart, the pain was too great to be borne, he cried out aloud, and started in his seat.

The little brown-faced woman at the further end of the carriage started too, and shrank into herself; he stared at her, bewildered.

It was so tragic, the gentle pathos of her face, as if she would beg forgiveness for her very existence; as if she would cry out to him not to crush her, as insects are crushed by the strong because they are unsightly.

He passed his hand across his eyes as if to clear his sight, and looked at her, puzzled.

"May I express my deep sympathy with the very sad story you have told me?" he said.

"My story? I have told you no story. I hope I do not disturb you. I have no right here I know;

mine is a third-class ticket, but the guard put me in here last time we stopped because the people in the carriage where I was were so noisy."

"I am amazed, bewildered," he said ; "certainly you told me your story."

The little woman had pride ; she set her lips firmly, and spoke coldly.

"I do not speak of my affairs to strangers," she said ; "even if they were of any interest I should not."

Her pride touched him more than all, it was so impotent, so gentle. He moved along the seat till he was opposite her, looking straight into the patient, proud, pathetic face ; he spoke tenderly, gently, and with infinite reverence.

"I am sure, though you have not told me your story, that the story which has in some strange way come within my knowledge is your story, and I want to hear the end. Do you mind telling me where you are going now ?"

"I am going to be a drudge among strangers. What is it to you ?"

What, indeed ? A little plain, faded woman, what did it mean that he, a man in the prime of life, handsome, rich, overburdened with friends, felt the tears rise in his eyes, and a great ache in his heart ? She might well look at him in wonder. He stretched out his hands towards her, he could scarcely speak.

"I know it all," he said, "I have felt it all. You

have suffered so much, you shall not suffer any more. I will make your life so bright to you if you will let me."

"I don't understand," she faltered.

"Neither do I," he cried, "neither do I, not how I know so much, or why I love you. I only know that I must take you right into my heart and keep you warm there, for I do love you!"

"Oh no! me, impossible!"

But looking in his eyes she saw that it was possible, and true, and she held out her hands, trembling, wondering, questioning. He answered the question with words that seemed to come through him, as if they were a message, and not only his own thought.

"Every human soul is lovable; we could not hold back from loving every soul on earth, could we once see it. But we cannot. Beauty hides the soul equally with deformity. To-day God has been very good to me: I have seen the soul of a woman and loved it."

"ANDREW PATERSON."

"ANDREW PATERSON."

SEYMOUR O'NEILL was fidgeting about in his smoky, untidy sitting room as restlessly as a woman, feeling more lonely in the last few moments of his pupil's absence than he had done all the fortnight he had been left alone. Richard Poole had wired to him, "Back some time to-day," but it was seven o'clock before a big ring at the bell, and the thud that followed as Dick flung himself against the door, to lean there comfortably till it was opened, announced his arrival.

O'Neill went to the door himself, peering at his young friend near-sightedly in the dark. He said—

"Well, here you are."

And Dick said, "Well, here I am."

And they went into the sitting-room together. Richard Poole looked round the room contentedly, and O'Neill looked at him very contentedly indeed now he had got him again.

" I'll go and tell them to serve dinner," he said.

"No, don't," said Dick. "Tell them to keep it back rather; I've a lot I want to say."

"Been—been—doing anything you shouldn't?"

O'Neill stammered over the question a little. If the boy had done anything wrong it would be he who would repent of it the most.

"Why, no," said Dick cheerfully; "one wouldn't say that. Something I should, I would call it. It all depends on the view you take of it."

O'Neill blinked at him tolerantly with his affectionate, near-sighted eyes. It was clear that any view he took would be a kindly and gentle one. He waited patiently.

"Well, I'm very glad to be back, Andrew Paterson," said Dick presently. He generally called his tutor "Andrew Paterson," he didn't know why; he had always heard him called so, and the name seemed to emphasise a sentence. There was a pause. Dick knew well enough what he wanted to say, but starting was difficult.

"Had a good time?" asked O'Neill, by way of helping him.

"Oh, yes. Good enough. That is, very good indeed."

"People all right?"

"I suppose so. I haven't seen them. I wasn't there."

"Oh! I thought you were."

"Yes, I mean't to go, but I went to the Dewhursts' first, and I liked it, and so I stayed on."

O'Neill said "Oh!" again, somewhat apprehensively this time. "A—a girl," he said, very nervously.

Dick burst out laughing.

"Yes, a girl," he said cheerfully. "Look here, Andrew Paterson, how long have I been here being reformed?"

"Six months," said the other.

"And the good advice you have given me in the time would fill several volumes as big as 'Mill's Logic,' wouldn't it?"

"Well," said O'Neill jealously, "you took most of it."

"I have taken all of it now," said Dick complacently. "You advised me to read, which I did, and not to spend money, which I didn't, and to be sober, which I have more or less, and to be vigilant, and all the rest of it; if we haven't gone all through the Christian virtues together, we've done our best at them."

"You've been a very good boy," said O'Neill, and he said it so lovingly that if Dick had had to confess that he had ceased to be a good boy it would have been a very bitter thing for both of them; but he had not, so he looked at his friend's anxious face and laughed.

"And all of the wise things you have ever said to me, Andrew Socrates Paterson, the wisest have been said on the engaging and all-important subject of love and matrimony."

O'Neill looked still more apprehensive.

"I said love was a serious thing, and not to be fooled over," he said.

"Exactly ; and you knew, you see, because you'd taken it seriously yourself. I've been thinking over what you said."

"I said that the love of a good woman was a good thing to get, worth getting, worth keeping when you'd got it, worth making sacrifices for."

" Now there I can't agree with you," said Dick ; " I don't see where the fun of making the sacrifices comes in. If you want to marry a girl you want to marry her *when* you want her, you know. What's the good of loving a girl because she's young and sweet, and then waiting till she is old and sour before you marry her? It's so hard on the girl. Oh yes, I've been thinking of that girl you are engaged to a great deal during the past fort-night. You told me she was a governess, you know. Governesses aren't very happy mostly, while you have a pretty jolly time. Don't you think it would have been far wiser to have married her right off, and brought her here, and let her have as good a time as she could along with us? I know you are trying to save money for her, but while you are doing it, she's spending all her youth ; getting no good out of being in love beyond a weekly illegible letter from you, and a visit when you can spare the time. Why, you know you have not been able to get up to see her these holidays. Fancy your not having one holiday together in the year. I've often pictured her to myself, waiting all alone patiently, pretty of course, but getting worn and old before her time."

O'Neill did not speak. He had been listening too earnestly to have an answer ready, but he ceased to think of his friend's affairs for a moment, and thought of his own. He half shut his eyes, and he smiled to himself a little: he had the air of one whose thoughts are very pleasant.

"What does all this lead us to?" he said after a while.

"Why, that if love is a good thing, as you say, and waiting is a bad thing, as I say, I've been very wise to marry right off, when we both wanted to."

O'Neill did not speak, but he looked so amazed, and at the same time so interested, that that was answer enough.

"She was staying with the Dewhursts," went on Dick, "such a very young girl, and awfully pretty. That was why I stayed; I couldn't leave her. I didn't think we should settle it as suddenly as this; but she was fond of me, that was what did it. She was so fond of me. I went a bit off my head to find a girl like that really caring for me. You see, I had been gone on her all the time—ever since I saw her, I mean. At first she seemed to like me—we got on capitally; so I stayed on, and it was very pleasant. Then she seemed to take a dislike to me—wouldn't come for walks, or go skating with me, and that sort of thing, and then, of course, I couldn't go till I had found out what was the matter, and the matter was—well, the matter was—she loved me."

Dick blushed over the last words, dwelling on them tenderly, and with a certain triumph. O'Neill no longer looked surprised, but attentive, and almost reverential. At the bottom of his heart the boy's love story seemed beautiful and sacred to him, only he was very anxious.

"This was how it all came about," Dick was saying. "She was going away next morning, and she thought no one was in the room. It was dark, and I didn't know she was there, I feeling pretty bad about her going. I was over by the fire, and she came in and went to the piano, in the dark, you know, and I did not feel as if I wanted to speak just then. Then she began to sing—a French thing; Mary Stuart's song, I believe it was. I didn't understand it, except '*Adieu, les plus beaux jours de ma vie*,' and there she broke down."

"Yes?"

"Why, then, you know, I found it easy enough to speak. I said everything there was to say, so did she, and the end of it was I ran up to town that night, and had a special licence ready by the time she came in the morning; and so we were married. I wonder what my father will say to my spending his Christmas tip on a wedding licence? I wonder if he can be persuaded to give me a wedding present in specie to make up for it?"

"You've not told him?"

"Oh, you'll do that, won't you?"

"I?"

"Yes; he'll take it so much better from you. You see, when I go home there's always a confession and a lecture, or a lecture without a confession. They'd take it for granted a thing was wrong if I told them I had done it, but they have such a high opinion of you that if you say it's all right they will believe it *is* all right. You've made them let me have my own way about going to the Bar, so you can make them let me have my own way about this."

"You've got it already."

"Yes, that's one comfort, they can't prevent it, so you must make them see it would be absurd to make a fuss now. They believe in you, you see. Do you remember how when I was first sent down here—in disgrace, don't you know——"

"You hadn't been doing anything very bad."

"No, but bad enough—knocking about, and spending money. Well, you remember when they gathered from my letters that I was pretty comfortable, they concluded naturally that you must therefore be 'even such a one as myself,' instead of a fit and proper tutor and guardian for me, and my father rushed down here to denounce you as a whited sepulchre because you couldn't but be a reprobate if I liked you, and found us peacefully reading Theocritus over the fire? I thought he was going to embrace me, or make you a present of fifty pounds, which would have been a far greater sign of affection. Blessings don't make such a hole in the parental banking account. You made my peace with him then."

"I told him that you were all right," said O'Neill, "and hadn't been any worse than most, and might turn out well if he'd exercise a little patience, that's all."

"Well, now you must tell him that I am all right, and have done rather *better* than most, and that everything will turn out very well indeed if he'll be good-natured," continued Dick.

"I'm not sure you aren't right," said O'Neill slowly; "I'm not sure this isn't the wisest thing you could have done. You want steadying; it will steady you."

"It will," said Dick quietly.

"You see you've got it in you to do something in the world, but you never had motive enough. Now a man couldn't have a better motive for getting on than a sweet young wife. She is a lady, of course?"

"Oh, yes, of course."

"You see the worst part of your character is your idleness. You know that you could do something if you liked, but you didn't care enough. Now you will care. You will feel bound to justify that girl's faith in you. You are an honourable man; you won't shirk a responsibility you have once undertaken. I think I can conscientiously say this to your people."

"That's what I want you to say."

O'Neill came across the room rug, and stood in front of the lad, looking into his face.

"It will be true, Dick?"

"Yes," said Dick; "it will be true."

"That's all right," said O'Neill, laying his hand on his shoulder for a moment. Then he gave a short, congratulatory laugh.

"So you're really married, and before me, too. Well, we neither of us expected that, did we? How long have you been a married man?"

"Three days."

"And you like it pretty well, eh?"

"Like it! Just wait till you see her, Andrew Paterson."

"Where have you left her?"

"Why, I haven't left her. Of course not. I brought her down here. You won't mind, will you? You see, I hadn't anywhere else to take her."

"Here?" And O'Neill looked round the room, blinking wonderingly as if he half-thought it possible that Mrs. Richard Poole had been in it all the time, and wondered he had not noticed her.

"She is waiting at the inn, and pretty tired she must have got of it while I have been talking. I may bring her round, mayn't I? There's plenty of room. There'll still be room when you bring your wife here too. You'll marry her soon, won't you, and then we'll all be cozy together? Why, what a good fellow you are, Andrew Paterson, you're looking quite pleased. I'll go and fetch her at once."

While he was gone, O'Neill muddled about the room moving things, not with any intention of making the place tidier in honour of the bride—he didn't perceive that it was untidy—but because he felt cheerful and restless.

"The best thing the boy could have done," he murmured; "the best thing he could have done, the very best; I'll tell his father so." Presently he heard Dick's step in the hall, and a moment later he burst into the room, followed by his bride, a pretty girl, shy and childish-looking.

"Seymour, old man, let me introduce you to my wife, she's been longing to meet you. Now look at her, and congratulate me, Andrew Paterson. Isn't she— Well, she's very white now, because she's tired travelling; but you shall see her to-morrow, after she has had a good rest."

"You must be very tired travelling, Mrs. Poole," O'Neill said hesitatingly.

"Very tired," she murmured. "Yes—very tired indeed."

“Get her a chair by the fire, Dick, and turn down that lamp a little; it is smoking.   I congratulate you both ; I hope you will be very happy.”

“She is tired,” said Dick ; “she generally has such a colour, but we have been travelling, and railways are always hateful. She has heard all about you,” he went on. “I have talked of you a great deal. In fact, she must know all your virtues by heart, I should say.”

“Why did you always call him Andrew Paterson ?” the girl asked.

“Why, I don’t know,” said Dick. “He was always called so, long before I knew him, and I’ve got into the way of it.”

“Some one once said that so shabby and uninteresting a person as I oughtn’t to have such a romantic name as Seymour O’Neill, and that I looked more like Andrew Paterson,” said O’Neill, carelessly. “So Andrew Paterson has stuck to me ever since. What does it matter? What does a name matter ?”

“It was a pity,” said the girl ; “it was a pity.”

“What does it matter?” said Dick cheerfully. “He’s just as good a fellow by one name as another, and Seymour O’Neill *is* a little highflown for every-day life. Now, Rosy, since you are here, and everything is explained, and settled, they might bring in dinner as soon as they like, mayn’t they, Andrew?”

“Tell them so,” said O’Neill. “They will want to see you ; they like you, you know.”

"Of course; I forgot, I promised old Margaret a bonnet for a Christmas present; I've got it in my hat-box. I'll tell the dear old woman that I'm a married man, and that she must give up her privilege of abusing me when I get wet through to Rosy now."

He flung out of the room. O'Neill waited till the door was shut, and then stumbled near-sightedly across towards the girl.

She was whiter than ever, and shrank back in her chair. What would he say or do? She was horribly frightened. Men killed faithless women sometimes; she had read of such things. He was close to her now. She was slipping from her chair to the floor, to cry for mercy or forgiveness; he laid a hand on her shoulder to stay her, and bent over her hesitating.

Whole volumes of excuse, of protest, of regret rose to her lips, but her lips could only tremble, not speak; she was not afraid after he had touched her. He was speaking.

"You must never let Dick know," he said; "I want you to understand that. He is a dear boy. We really liked each other, you know; and I think if he found out what he had done, he would kill himself."

"Here's the dinner," cried Dick at the door. "Oh, I didn't notice I'd turned the lamp down as far as that; it's quite dark in here. Rosy, old Margaret will show you upstairs to take your hat off! but be quick down, that's a good child. Isn't she sweet, old man? You may praise her now she isn't here, you know."

"Quite the prettiest girl I ever saw," said O'Neill.

"You think so, really? Well, that's nice of you, when you are engaged yourself. But what's wrong? You look upset. Feel a bit 'left,' don't you, or as if it ought to be your wife who was here?"

"I think I'd better tell you," said O'Neill slowly. "I wasn't going to talk about it just yet. I didn't want to spoil your first evening with bad news. The fact is, I think after I have made this right with your father I shall go abroad a bit. My marriage won't come off, Dick. She—the girl, you know—is dead; she died a few days ago. Hush! here is your wife. Please don't speak of it to her, it would distress her."

Jarrold and Sons, Printers, Norwich, Yarmouth, and London.

Opinions of the Press

ON

WORKS BY CURTIS YORKE.

Crown 8vo, Cloth, 3/6 each.   (Postage 4½d.)

HUSH ! 3/6

" Curtis Yorke's work is fresh and bright, and the story is told with singular depth of insight and delicacy of feeling."—*Whitehall Review.*

" 'HUSH' is in many ways a remarkable novel, and from every point of view superior to the current fiction of the day."—*Morning Post.*

" 'HUSH' is a clever story."—*Standard.*

" Curtis Yorke always writes bright and readable novels. Told with considerable vigour and pathos."—*Spectator.*

" Curtis Yorke, the author of 'HUSH,' may be congratulated on having produced a very readable novel. The interest is well sustained throughout."—*Daily Telegraph.*

" The book is one that should be read."—*Athenæum.*

" The story is well told."—*Graphic.*

THAT LITTLE GIRL. 3/6

" This is a novel of considerable spirit and interest. The tone of the story is throughout everything that we could wish."—*Spectator.*

" A very charming and well-written story."—*Queen.*

" Cannot fail to charm the most fastidious."—*Court Journal.*

" A brighter, pleasanter book it would not be easy to find."—*Manchester Examiner.*

" A pleasant novel is 'THAT LITTLE GIRL,' in a style that is bright, fresh, and original."—*Lady's Pictorial.*

" It is a real pleasure to come across such a novel as this."—*Reciter and Speaker.*

" The story is an excellent one, showing much originality both in conception and execution."—*Bookseller.*

London: Jarrold & Sons, 10 & 11, Warwick Lane.
And of all Booksellers.

DUDLEY.

3/6

"A romance of more than usual interest; it is highly original, the incidents are unusual, and the situations fresh and ingenious."—*Bookseller*.

"It is sometime since such a fresh, pleasant book has come under our notice as ' DUDLEY.' "—*Whitehall Review*.

"Certain to please a large circle of readers."—*Graphic*.

"The novel is decidedly interesting."—*Court Journal*.

"'DUDLEY' is undoubtedly a clever and interesting novel, powerfully worked out."—*Glasgow Herald*.

"A bright, well-written story of present day life, which we have read with sustained interest to the end."—*Inquirer*.

"Decidedly original."—*Morning Post*.

"One of the best novels of the week."—*Scotsman*.

"The author writes in a pleasant, lively fashion, and tells a story very prettily."—*Athenæum*.

"'DUDLEY' is a charming love story."—*Literary World*.

"The story is a well-written and interesting one. The book is published in one volume, but has more in it and is better worth reading than the majority of three-volume novels."—*Vanity Fair*.

THE BROWN PORTMANTEAU, 3 6

And other Stories.

"The stories are all interesting, and the volume is sure of a welcome."—*Literary World*.

"The writer is natural, realistic, and entertaining."—*Morning Post*.

"Told in a rapid and effective fashion without analysis or comment, as stories of incident should be told."—*Athenæum*.

"Most attractive reading."—*Norwich Mercury*.

"Touch the deepest mysteries of mind and life, and display a literary ability of a high order."—*Christian Age*.

"Clever stories, short, and pithy."—*Publishers' Circular*.

London: Jarrold & Sons, 10 & 11, Warwick Lane.

And of all Booksellers.

THE WILD RUTHVENS.   _{3 6}

"The book is most amusing."—*Manchester Guardian.*

"An enchanting work. The story runs on with happy, blithesome tread to the end, which is reached all too soon.'—*St. Stephen's Review.*

"It is wonderful what a variety of incident the author has managed to interweave into the story."—*Bradford Observer.*

"'THE WILD RUTHVENS' secure our interest at the outset, and retain it to the end."—*Glasgow Herald.*

"'THE WILD RUTHVENS' is likely to be a great favourite . . . . irresistibly taking . . . . inexpressibly touching. and, as a pathetic picture, has not been often surpassed."—*Life.*

"Will not only sustain, but widen the reputation which this author has won. It is full of movement and colour."—*Publishers' Circular.*

"The book has an amount of 'go' about it which proves the capacity of Curtis Yorke to tell a rattling story."—*Dundee Advertiser.*

A ROMANCE OF MODERN LONDON.   _{3'6}

"This is a sweet and wholesome story, and comes as an immense relief after the common run of circulating library novels."—*Pictorial World.*

"We cannot but praise this story as far and away above the average of modern novels."—*Whitehall Review.*

"The story is told throughout not only with great cleverness, but with unusual delicacy and tenderness."—*Guardian.*

"Interest in the work never flags."—*Scotsman.*

"Entertaining and interesting: a book which it is a thorough recreation to read."—*Manchester Examiner.*

"Considerable ingenuity of construction, as well as much really clever writing, is to be found in Curtis Yorke's new novel."—*Court Journal.*

London: Jarrold & Sons, 10 & 11, Warwick Lane.

And of all Booksellers.

ONCE.

3/6

"Few three-volume novels contain such forcible and effective writing as we find in Curtis Yorke's story, 'ONCE.' We are sure that 'Once' will find plenty of readers among those who are on the look out for a good story."—*Literary World.*

"'ONCE' is quite as good as any of this author's previous novels, and that is not faint praise."—*The Scotsman.*

"Curtis Yorke's style is always fresh, clear, and interesting.'—*Manchester Examiner.*

"Full in incident, rich in pathos and passion, and told in fascinating language, 'ONCE' will be warmly appreciated by all lovers of fiction."—*Christian Age.*

"'ONCE' by Curtis Yorke, is a powerfully written story, in which the vicissitudes of the dominant passion are related in a manner so as to at once take possession of the reader's attention. 'Once' will form a fit companion for the author's other writings; he who have read them will make a point to read this."—*Suffolk Chronicle.*

"A domestic story of modern life . . . so cleverly contrived that the enthralled reader remains interested to the end."—*Weekly Citizen.*

"'ONCE,' a story showing all Curtis Yorke's capacity for vigorous and vivid writing, and for skilful construction of plot."—*The Scottish Leader.*

"'ONCE' is distinctly an exceptional novel."—*Newcastle Daily Leader.*

"'ONCE' is much above the average of present-day fiction."—*Dundee Advertiser.*

"The novel is far above the average, and is worthy of the pen of the author of 'Hush' and 'Dudley.'"—*Perthshire Advertiser.*

"The tale is vividly and well told."—*Bath Herald.*

"'ONCE' may fairly be said to keep the reader's interest on the *qui vive* through the 300 pages occupied in telling the story."—*Freeman's Journal.*

"The story retains the interest of the reader from first to last. It is original in its conception and its situations, and while in many parts full of pathos, yet it is not without its humours."—*Belfast Evening Telegraph.*

London: Jarrold & Sons, 10 & 11, Warwick Lane.
And of all Booksellers.

Selections from Jarrold & Sons' New Books, &c.

Leaves from the Log Of a Gentleman Gipsy:

IN WAYSIDE CAMP AND CARAVAN.

By GORDON STABLES, M.D., C.M., R.N.

*Author of " The People's A B C Guide to Health,"
" The Cruise of the Land Yacht ' Wanderer,'" "Sickness or Health ?
or, the Danger of Trifling Ailments," " Health upon Wheels," &c.*

Demy 8vo, 460 pages, Price 15/-.

With 56 Illustrations by Dewey Bates and Alfred Hardy.

The Times says:—" We can commend his book to those who share, or would fain imitate his tastes."

The St. James' Gazette says:—" There is not a dull page from cover to cover."

The Girl's Own Book of Health and Beauty.

By GORDON STABLES, M.D, C.M., R.N.,

*Author of " Sickness or Health ?" " The People's A B C Guide to Health,"
" Leaves from the Log of a Gentleman Gipsy, in Wayside Camp
and Caravan," &c.*

Crown 8vo, 248 pp., cloth, 2/6.

EXTRACT FROM PREFACE.—" I desire to teach my girl readers how to be healthy, because there can be no beauty without health. Brightness of eyes, clearness of complexion, and happiness of expression belong only to the possessor of health. A girl who is but indifferently well, is self-conscious, ill-at-ease in society, not clear in eyes, and very sallow as to skin."

The Leicester Chronicle says:—" Teems with useful hints and good suggestions. Ought to be n the hands of every young woman."

The Dundee Advertiser says :—"A series of readable papers, giving in the least technical language a great deal of valuable information in an interesting way "

Selections from Jarrold & Sons' New Books, &c.

Uniform with the " Girl's Own Book of Health and Beauty."

Crown 8vo, 220 pages, cloth, 2/6.

The Boys' Book of Health and Strength.

By GORDON STABLES, M.D., C.M.
(SURGEON ROYAL NAVY.)

Author of the " Girl's Own Book of Health and Beauty,"
" Sickness or Health,"
" The People's A B C Guide to Health,"
" Leaves from the Log of a Gentleman Gipsy—In Wayside Camp and
Caravan," " Health upon Wheels," etc.

EXTRACT FROM PREFACE.—

" Hardly anyone, unconnected to a large extent with boys and boy life, could believe how much and how often boys think about their health, their growth, their appearance, and looks. Boys too often want guidance in their young lives, and although this is guessed at by teachers and pastors, and much good advice given, such advice, though beneficial on the whole, cannot be made to suit individual cases. These boys are shy and sensitive, and in their troubles will steer clear of a consultation with a teacher, a clergyman, or doctor. Yet by letter they will freely consult their editor, whom they look upon as that friend in need that he truly is. As to consulting parents, this in the present day would hardly ever be dreamed of by a boy, and the parent himself is nearly always too busy in the struggle for existence to tender unasked-for advice."

BY THE SAME AUTHOR.

Uniform with the " Boys' Book of Health and Strength," and the " Girl's
Own Book of Health and Beauty."

Second Edition.   Crown 8vo, 287 pages, cloth, 2/6.

Sickness or Health? A Question for Everybody; or the Danger of Trifling Ailments.

Literary World says: "'Sickness or Health?' is an excellent book in every way, and we trust its success will be equal to its merits."

The Christian says: "Instead of giving medical prescriptions that may be wrongly applied, the author of this work gives much sound advice of all-round application."

LONDON : JARROLD & SONS, 10 & 11, WARWICK LANE, E.C.

And of all Booksellers.